Playing to Win at Bridge

Playing to Win at Bridge. a selection of entertaining and instructive problems from actual play, was originally published in 1976 and has been reprinted five times. This is a revised and up-dated edition with a number of new problems added.

For each problem two hands are shown together with the bidding and the play to the first few tricks. The reader is then invited to take over and plan the play or defence before turning to the solution where all four hands are given.

As one would expect from a master teacher, the emphasis is on practical problems of the sort that are frequently encountered in a game. In the handling of these common situations lies the secret of playing to win.

Ron Klinger is not only an international player, a winner of many prestigious bridge championships and a well-known leading bridge journalist. He is also a Master of Laws, with First Class Honours, and has years of experience in teaching bridge at all levels. He brings to his books the sharpness of a trained legal mind, together with the authority of a Grand Master and the understanding of a top teacher.

'**Playing to Win at Bridge** *is as good a quiz book as has ever appeared. The feature that distinguishes this collection from most others is the absence of special themes. Instead of examples of well known ideas, the author presents truly practical situations. As declarer, you are more likely to be wondering how best to combine the different chances than how to operate an esoteric squeeze. On defence, you must worry about your aces getting away before you turn your thoughts to complex coups. In short, the questions emphasise those aspects of bridge play that are truly important at the table.*
Our quibbles with the analysis are minor, and we recommend the book as outstanding of its kind'
—The Bridge World

Ron Klinger

Playing to Win at Bridge

Practical Problems for the Improving Player

VICTOR GOLLANCZ

in association with

PETER CRAWLEY

First published in Great Britain 1976
in association with Peter Crawley
by Victor Gollancz Ltd
Sixth impression 1992
This new edition first published 1999
in association with Peter Crawley
by Victor Gollancz
An imprint of Orion Books Ltd
Orion House, 5 Upper Saint Martin's Lane, London WC2H 9EA

A catalogue record for this book
is available from the British Library

ISBN 0 575 06736 5

Typeset in Australia by Modern Bridge Publications,
60 Kameruka Road, Northbridge, NSW 2063, Australia

Printed in Great Britain by
Clays Ltd, St Ives plc

Contents

A competent player should score at least 90% in this section and should not require more than two or three minutes to come up with the winning line for each problem.

A competent player should score at least 75% in this section and should not require more than three or four minutes to come up with the winning line for each problem. A strong player should score 90%.

The problems in the final section are assessed as fairly difficult. The average player will be doing well to score better than 50%. To obtain maximum benefit, you should make a genuine effort to solve the problems. Although they are not simple, each question admits of a logical answer and the necessary clues are to be found in the bidding and early play.

INTRODUCTION

Bridge skill is based to a great extent on experience. No amount of theoretical study and technical knowledge can make up for the failure to recognise the problem presented by a new deal. The advantage of the player who 'has been there before' is considerable; the experienced player has an immense storehouse of familiar situations on which to draw.

This collection aims to equip the less experienced player with the everyday situations of rubber and tournament bridge in order to add to that storehouse. Having met a situation here and having grasped the reasoning involved, a player will be able to deal with similar problems when they actually arise.

You will not find esoteric deals or complex squeeze positions, standard textbook hands or 'sure trick' plays, which though important, occur only rarely at the table. Rather, you may expect the countless, irritating problems which crop up every day, and the clues by which they may be solved. This is a book of practical problems taken from real life. You may take comfort from the fact that on almost every hand somebody went wrong, failing to make the contract or failing to find the best defence.

There is no common thread running through the hands. You will not see one section devoted to endplays, another to trump control, a third to card-reading, and so on. That is not what happens at the bridge table where there is no rhyme or reason to the order in which problems occur. The hands are intended to simulate normal playing conditions, although you have the advantage of knowing that you face a problem on each deal. At the table, one of the hardest things is to recognise that a problem exists. The world is full of expert dummy players and brilliant defenders five seconds after the play of the hand is over. It is the ability to solve the problem five seconds *before* the critical moment that is the hallmark of the top player.

The bidding is almost invariably presented as it happened at the table. The opponents' bidding is often less than perfect and at times frankly shocking, but isn't that what happens in real life? Thank heavens we do not sit down to play against world champions all the time. Similarly, the contracts reached by you and your partner are not always ideal and your bidding sequences are not always what they should be, but then you and your present partner are not the world's best bidders, are you? (If you *are* the world's best bidders, please assume that you have been asked to play the hand for someone else.)

Particulars of dealer, vulnerability and setting are given for each problem along with the actual play up to the critical point. Where any additional information about the actual auction is required, it is provided. That does not mean that all additional information is relevant. As happens at the table, you receive a lot of excess information and you have to sift out from the available data what is relevant and what is not. Is it the bidding by the opponents? Is it partner's lead? Is it the way declarer is tackling the hand? Is it partner's signalling? Or is it just a matter of knowing your card combinations?

The elements of good declarer play and competent defence are similar to the elements of good detective work. Sherlock Holmes would have made a splendid bridge player, for he had the ability to sort out from a morass of clues those few that pointed towards the correct solution. Facility in logical reasoning is a matter of training and practice. At some time in the future, after bringing in a difficult contract or pulling off a tough defence, you may find yourself saying, 'Elementary, my dear partner!'

A word is needed about the presentation of the problems. Where a card is shown in **bold face** it means that the trick was won with that card. When a discard is made or when someone ruffs, this is indicated in *italics*. For each trick the player who makes the lead is given first, followed by the next three cards in rotation. For example:

South leads $\diamond$ **K:** two, three, seven

This means that South led the king of diamonds and won the trick (**bold face**) and that West played the two, North the three and East the seven of diamonds. Here is an actual problem, No. 44:

♠ J 10 5 3
♡ 8 6 5 2
◇ 5
♣ A 10 4 3

WEST	NORTH	EAST	SOUTH
			1NT*
No	No	No	
*12-14 points			

♠ Q 9 7 4
♡ K Q 9
◇ K J 8 7
♣ K 6

The play:
1 West leads ♣5: three, **king,** eight
2 East leads ◇7: **queen,** ten, five
3 **South leads ♠A:** eight, three, seven
4 **South leads ♠K:** *West discards ♣2*
5 South leads ♠6: *West discards ◇3,* ♠J from dummy . . .

How should East defend?

Presenting the above in detail: West leads the five of clubs, the three is played from dummy, East wins with the king (**bold**) and South follows with the eight. East returns the seven of diamonds and the trick is won by South's queen, West playing the ten and dummy the five. South plays off the ace and king of spades and West discards the two of clubs on the second round. Then comes a spade to dummy's jack, West discarding the three of diamonds, and at this point you are asked to plan the defence from East's point of view.

After a little practice you should have no trouble in following the play on each hand. It is a good idea to use paper and pencil when tackling each problem and to write down a definite answer. This will give a better indication of your accuracy than the inflated idea you may acquire by simply thinking about possible lines of play, then looking at the answer and saying to yourself, 'Oh, yes, of course that's what I would have done.' Your aim should be improved technique, not self-delusion.

I hope you enjoy the challenge presented by the problems, including the sixteen new ones. I know you will be a better player after studying them.

Ron Klinger
1999

PART 1: Elementary Level

1
Dealer North,
both sides vulnerable.

♠ 8 3
♡ Q 10 3
◇ Q 7 6 2
♣ 9 8 3 2

WEST	NORTH	EAST	SOUTH
	No	No	2NT
No	3NT	All pass	

```
        N
  W           E
        S
```

♠ A K 6
♡ A K J 4
◇ J 4
♣ K Q J 5

The play :
1 West leads the ♠Q: three, two . . .

Plan South's play.

2

♠ J 7 6 2
♡ J 9
◇ K 5 4 3
♣ A 6 2

Pairs, dealer North,
neither side vulnerable.

♠ A K 10 4
♡ K 6
◇ J 8 7
♣ 9 7 5 3

```
        N
  W           E
        S
```

WEST	NORTH	EAST	SOUTH
	No	No	1♡
1♠	1NT	No	3♡
No	4♡	All pass	

The play :
1 **West leads the ♠A:** two, three, five
2 West leads the ♣7: **ace,** eight, ten
3 The ♡J is led from dummy: eight, two, **king.**

Plan West's defence.

1. Maximizing your chances

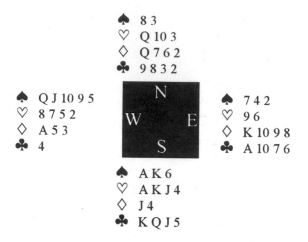

Trap 1 : Don't duck the opening lead. It would be all right to do so if you could be sure of a spade continuation, but if the defence were to switch to diamonds you could lose one spade, three diamonds and a club.

Trap 2 : After winning the ace of spades, don't play the king of clubs. That would cost a trick if East began with the ace of clubs singleton.

The correct line is to win the ace of spades, play the four of hearts to dummy's 10 and lead a low club, playing the king if East plays low. Then:

a) if the king loses to the ace, play the queen of clubs when you regain the lead and claim if the clubs are 3-2. If East began with 10-x-x-x in clubs, play the jack of hearts, overtake with dummy's queen and lead the 9 of clubs for a finesse;

b) if the king of clubs holds, do *not* play the jack of hearts to lead another club from dummy; that would fail on the layout above. Instead, lay down the queen of clubs. If East has four clubs and takes the ace, you later cross to the queen of hearts and run the 9 of clubs. If East lets the queen of clubs win, you will cross at once to the queen of hearts and lead another club.

2. The sins of the auction may be visited upon the defence

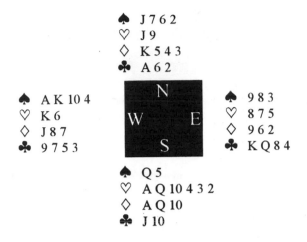

```
                    ♠ J 7 6 2
                    ♡ J 9
                    ◇ K 5 4 3
                    ♣ A 6 2
                          N
    ♠ A K 10 4                        ♠ 9 8 3
    ♡ K 6           W          E      ♡ 8 7 5
    ◇ J 8 7                           ◇ 9 6 2
    ♣ 9 7 5 3             S           ♣ K Q 8 4
                    ♠ Q 5
                    ♡ A Q 10 4 3 2
                    ◇ A Q 10
                    ♣ J 10
```

One of the most difficult areas of defence is that pertaining to the cashing of defensive tricks in the right order. It takes close cooperation and accurate count signals to make sure that the defenders cash all the tricks that are available. It will repay most partnerships to spend some time clarifying their agreements in this area.

Here it is important for West to cash the ace of spades before leading a second club. If West returns a club immediately South is likely to make four hearts. East will win and, placing West with five spades for the 1♠ overcall, will almost certainly try to cash another club. South will ruff the third club and declarer's other spade loser will disappear on the thirteenth diamond.

West can be confident that the ace of spades will survive, for if East had started with Q-x-x-x in spades and a strong club holding (evident from the eight of clubs signal), East would have competed with two spades over one no trump.

3
Dealer South,
neither side vulnerable.

♠ J 3
♡ 6 4
◇ Q J 10 6 3
♣ A K J 6

WEST	NORTH	EAST	SOUTH
			1NT
No	3NT	All pass	

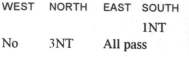

♠ A 10 5
♡ Q J
◇ A 8 4 2
♣ Q 4 3 2

The final contract is a little inelegant, but all is not lost since West leads the ♠4. How do you play to maximize your chances of success?

Plan South's play.

4

♠ K Q J 4
♡ Q 8 5
◇ Q 10 7 4 3
♣ 9

Dealer North,
both sides vulnerable.

♠ 8 6 2
♡ 9
◇ 8 5
♣ A Q 8 7 6 4 3

WEST	NORTH	EAST	SOUTH
	No	No	1♠
3♣*	3♠	No	4♠
No	No	No	

*Weak jump-overcall

The play:
1 West leads the ♡9: five, **ace,** six
2 East returns the ♡10: seven, **ruffed with the ♠6,** eight.

How should West continue?

5

Teams, dealer North,
both sides vulnerable.

♠ J 9 3
♡ A K Q J
♢ 9 6 2
♣ A K Q

WEST	NORTH	EAST	SOUTH
	1♡	No	1NT
No	3NT	All pass	

♠ A 7 4
♡ 6 5 3
♢ J 8 7
♣ J 8 3 2

West leads the ♠6. Plan the play.

6

♠ K Q 7 2
♡ 8
♢ A Q J 7 3
♣ K 10 7

Teams, dealer East,
North-South vulnerable.

♠ 8 6 4
♡ K 9 7 6 3
♢ K 9 6
♣ 9 5

WEST	NORTH	EAST	SOUTH
		No	No
No	1♢	No	2NT
No	3NT	All pass	

The play:

1 West leads the ♡6: eight, **ace, four**
2 East returns the ♡J: South plays the queen . . .

Plan West's defence.

3. Out of the rut

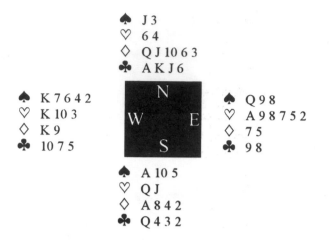

```
                 ♠ J 3
                 ♡ 6 4
                 ◊ Q J 10 6 3
                 ♣ A K J 6
♠ K 7 6 4 2          N          ♠ Q 9 8
♡ K 10 3        W       E       ♡ A 9 8 7 5 2
◊ K 9                           ◊ 7 5
♣ 10 7 5            S           ♣ 9 8
                 ♠ A 10 5
                 ♡ Q J
                 ◊ A 8 4 2
                 ♣ Q 4 3 2
```

The routine play is a low spade from dummy in order to ensure two
tricks in the suit, but the desperate heart situation calls for other
measures. If the diamond finesse is working you'll have no problems,
but what if the finesse fails? You want to encourage West to continue
spades rather than to find the heart switch.

Suppose you play the three of spades from dummy at trick one. Whether
East plays the queen or the eight, West will be able to work out that you
have a double stopper in spades. And when you cross to the ace of clubs
for the diamond finesse, West is likely to realise that you will make at
least nine tricks as soon as you regain the lead. West will therefore
switch to hearts, carefully unblocking the ten in the process.

But if you play the jack of spades from dummy and win East's queen
with the ace, West will find it irresistible to infer that the ten is with
East. On winning the king of diamonds, West will underlead the king of
spades in order to avoid blocking the suit.

Keep an eye on West's face as you win with the ten. It will be a moment
to cherish.

4. Trust your partner, but safety first

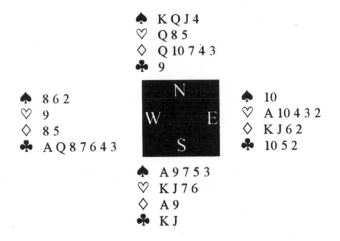

```
                    ♠  K Q J 4
                    ♡  Q 8 5
                    ◇  Q 10 7 4 3
                    ♣  9
   ♠  8 6 2              N           ♠  10
   ♡  9            W         E       ♡  A 10 4 3 2
   ◇  8 5                            ◇  K J 6 2
   ♣  A Q 8 7 6 4 3      S           ♣  10 5 2
                    ♠  A 9 7 5 3
                    ♡  K J 7 6
                    ◇  A 9
                    ♣  K J
```

West should cash the ace of clubs before playing a diamond.

East's ♡10 return is a suit-preference request for a diamond return, but that does not mean East must have the ace or that West should blindly follow instructions.

South is known to have started with K J x x in hearts (East's ace at trick one places the king with South, and the ten at trick two marks South with the jack). You can visualize what will happen on a diamond return if East does not have the ace. South will win, draw trumps in two rounds, and discard dummy's club on the fourth heart. The contract will thus make if South can hold the diamond losers to one.

Cashing the club ace first is perfectly safe. The diamonds can wait, since South can have no way of disposing of any losers in that suit.

Yes, five clubs is a good East-West contract, succeeding unless the opponents lead trumps initially, but this is no reason to let them make four spades.

5. Don't be an automaton

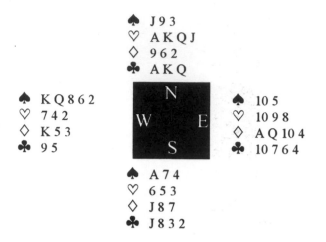

```
            ♠ J 9 3
            ♡ A K Q J
            ◇ 9 6 2
            ♣ A K Q

♠ K Q 8 6 2                    ♠ 10 5
♡ 7 4 2        N               ♡ 10 9 8
◇ K 5 3    W       E           ◇ A Q 10 4
♣ 9 5          S               ♣ 10 7 6 4

            ♠ A 7 4
            ♡ 6 5 3
            ◇ J 8 7
            ♣ J 8 3 2
```

Normally the correct play with J-9-x in dummy opposite A-x or A-x-x is to insert dummy's nine. This caters for the more frequent situations: West is more likely to have led from K-10-x-x-x or Q-10-x-x-x than from K-Q-x-x-x.

But circumstances alter cases. Here, if West has led from K-10-x-x-x or Q-10-x-x-x, you cannot, barring miracles, make the contract. East's honour will force out the ♠A, your only entry, before the clubs can be unblocked. After winning the ♠A you can try returning a spade, of course, but only the rawest beginner in West seat will play low. As you will have nine tricks if ♠J wins, West will naturally win the spade and switch to diamonds, putting you one down.

Your only legitimate chance is that West has led from the king and queen of spades, and you should therefore play the jack from dummy. If it wins, play off dummy's clubs, come to hand with the ♠A, and cash ♣J and the hearts for nine tricks.

If the ♠J is covered by East, you will have to play for the miracle layout. Duck in hand, win the spade return if it comes, cash dummy's club and heart winners and play a diamond hoping for East's hand to be ♠Q x ♡ x x x x ◇A K Q ♣ x x x x.

6. Out for a duck

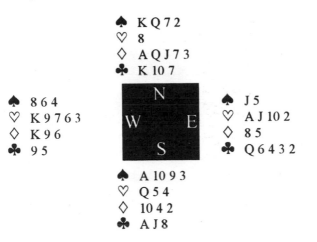

```
                  ♠  K Q 7 2
                  ♡  8
                  ◇  A Q J 7 3
                  ♣  K 10 7
   ♠  8 6 4           N          ♠  J 5
   ♡  K 9 7 6 3                  ♡  A J 10 2
   ◇  K 9 6      W       E       ◇  8 5
   ♣  9 5                        ♣  Q 6 4 3 2
                     S
                  ♠  A 10 9 3
                  ♡  Q 5 4
                  ◇  10 4 2
                  ♣  A J 8
```

Sometimes it is correct to duck in defence in order to preserve
communications with partner, but this isn't one of those times. If you
duck, you can see the declarer making at least nine tricks and the
contract. South will make one heart, five diamonds (since the finesse is
working) and at least three tricks in the black suits even in the unlikely
event that partner has an ace.

The tricks to defeat the contract must be taken now or not at all. You
must win the king of hearts and continue the suit. If South began with
Q-10-x or Q-10-x-x in hearts there is nothing you can do about it.

After the hand you may compliment East on the proper return of the
♡J. The careless return of the ♡2 ('to give you the count, partner')
would have blocked the suit.

It would of course be poor form to ask 'innocently' if North and South
could have made six spades.

7

Teams, dealer West,
North-South vulnerable.

	♠	7
	♡	K J 4
	◇	A 10 8 3 2
	♣	A 7 4 2

WEST	NORTH	EAST	SOUTH
3♣	3◇	No	4NT
No	5♡	No	6NT
No	No	No	

```
        N
    W       E
        S
```

	♠	K Q J 10
	♡	A Q 3
	◇	K J 9 4
	♣	K 6

The play:

1 West leads the ♣Q: two, *East discards ♡2*, **king**
2 South leads the ♠K: **East wins with the ♠A**
3 East returns the ♠5: West follows . . .

Plan South's play.

8

♠	J 9 5
♡	K 8 4 2
◇	K J 7 6
♣	Q 6

Rubber, dealer South,
both sides vulnerable.

♠	8 3
♡	Q J 6 5
◇	A 8 3
♣	10 9 8 4

```
        N
    W       E
        S
```

WEST	NORTH	EAST	SOUTH
			1♠
No	2◇	No	3♠
No	4♠	All pass	

The play:

1 West leads the ♣10: queen, **king,** two
2 East returns the ♠4: six, eight, **jack**
3 The ◇6 is led from dummy: five, queen, **ace.**

How should West proceed?

9
Dealer East,
both sides vulnerable.

♠ K 9
♡ A Q 7 5 3
◇ K 6
♣ A 6 4 3

WEST	NORTH	EAST	SOUTH
		No	2♠*
No	4♠	All pass	

*weak two

♠ A Q 10 8 3 2
♡ 6 2
◇ J 5 3 2
♣ 8

The play:
1 West leads the ♠6: nine, jack, **ace.**

Plan the play.

10
Rubber, dealer South,
both sides vulnerable.

♠ 10 9 5
♡ J 10 3 2
◇ A 7
♣ K Q J 10

WEST	NORTH	EAST	SOUTH
			1NT*
No	3NT	All pass	

*15-17

♠ J 8 3
♡ A 9 6 5
◇ K J 8
♣ A 7 3

The play:
West leads ◇3: seven from dummy . . .

Plan East's defence.

7. A sure thing

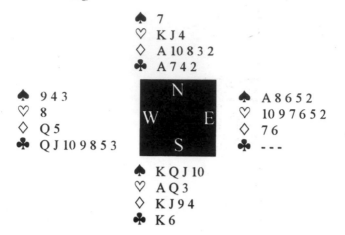

```
                  ♠  7
                  ♡  K J 4
                  ◇  A 10 8 3 2
                  ♣  A 7 4 2

  ♠  9 4 3            N              ♠  A 8 6 5 2
  ♡  8                               ♡  10 9 7 6 5 2
  ◇  Q 5         W         E         ◇  7 6
  ♣  Q J 10 9 8 5 3                  ♣  - - -
                     S

                  ♠  K Q J 10
                  ♡  A Q 3
                  ◇  K J 9 4
                  ♣  K 6
```

A little knowledge is a dangerous thing. Thinking 'Aha, West has shown up with seven clubs and two spades, so he must be short in diamonds', the declarer played a diamond to the ace and finessed through East on the way back. Ouch! One down.

Perhaps it would be more accurate to say that little knowledge is a dangerous thing. Although the odds favour East having length in diamonds, why accept any odds when the contract can be ensured simply by playing off your spades and hearts and finding out *exactly* how many diamonds West has?

On the actual hand, West shows out on the fourth spade and on the second heart. With seven clubs marked from trick one, that leaves precisely two diamonds. If West proved to have only three cards in the major suits, you would know to play West for three diamonds. If West showed up with five cards in the majors it would be equally clear that East would have three or four diamonds.

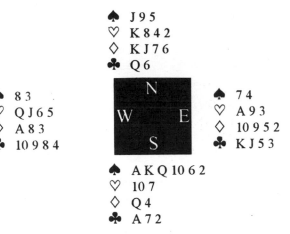

```
            ♠ J 9 5
            ♡ K 8 4 2
            ◇ K J 7 6
            ♣ Q 6
  ♠ 8 3                      ♠ 7 4
  ♡ Q J 6 5       N          ♡ A 9 3
  ◇ A 8 3     W       E      ◇ 10 9 5 2
  ♣ 10 9 8 4      S          ♣ K J 5 3
            ♠ A K Q 10 6 2
            ♡ 10 7
            ◇ Q 4
            ♣ A 7 2
```

You must switch to the queen of hearts at trick four. If the declarer has the ace of hearts, you will not beat four spades, for South will make six spade tricks (the jump to three spades should be based on a six-card suit), two hearts and two diamonds. The only losers then would be two clubs and a diamond.

On anything but the heart return declarer has an easy time, discarding a heart loser on the diamonds and ruffing the third club on the table. You don't know that East does have ♡A, but you do know you will not beat four spades if not.

Perhaps you also noted South as a possible future partner. That careful duck at trick one was a precautionary measure which would have ensured the success of the contract if East had held the ace of diamonds. By ducking, declarer aims to prevent West, the danger hand, from regaining the lead at a later stage to play a heart through the king. If declarer fails to duck and East does win with the ace of diamonds, East could put partner in by underleading the jack of clubs.

9. Backing the favourite

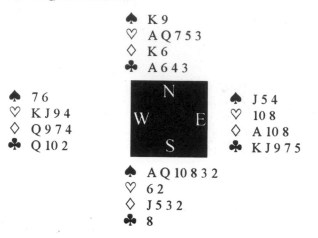

```
                    ♠  K 9
                    ♡  A Q 7 5 3
                    ◇  K 6
                    ♣  A 6 4 3
  ♠  7 6                              ♠  J 5 4
  ♡  K J 9 4          N               ♡  10 8
  ◇  Q 9 7 4     W        E           ◇  A 10 8
  ♣  Q 10 2           S               ♣  K J 9 7 5
                    ♠  A Q 10 8 3 2
                    ♡  6 2
                    ◇  J 5 3 2
                    ♣  8
```

A sound start is to count your tricks as declarer. You have eight via six spades and two aces. A successful heart finesse will bring in one extra and if either the ace or the queen of diamonds is well-placed, you can generate a trick there. Do not count on a diamond ruff. A second trump lead when the opponents gain the lead in diamonds will put paid to that.

Definitely try the hearts first. If the heart finesse is on, you can probably bring in enough tricks without resorting to the diamonds. Because you wish to take advantage of dummy's length in hearts, you should start on hearts without playing another round of trumps. The king of spades may be a useful entry to return to dummy.

At trick two, play a heart to the queen. When it wins, cash the ace of hearts and ruff a heart. A spade to dummy and another heart ruff sets up dummy's last heart as a winner. Draw the missing trump, cross to the ace of clubs and discard a diamond loser on the heart winner.

If the heart finesse loses and a trump comes back, you win, cash the ace of hearts and ruff a heart. If hearts are 3-3, again you are home without touching diamonds. If the hearts are not 3-3, draw the missing trump(s) and lead a diamond. If West has the ace of diamonds and the hearts were 4-2 originally, you will still be smiling when the hand is over.

10. Partner's bust stands out

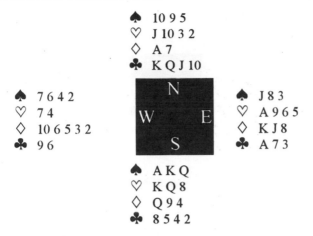

```
              ♠ 10 9 5
              ♡ J 10 3 2
              ◇ A 7
              ♣ K Q J 10

♠ 7 6 4 2                        ♠ J 8 3
♡ 7 4          N                 ♡ A 9 6 5
◇ 10 6 5 3 2   W   E             ◇ K J 8
♣ 9 6              S             ♣ A 7 3

              ♠ A K Q
              ♡ K Q 8
              ◇ Q 9 4
              ♣ 8 5 4 2
```

East should play the jack of diamonds, not the king.

West cannot hold a point, for dummy has 11, East has 13 and South's opening showed 15-17 points (West might have one jack but for the fact that East can see all four of them). The one card of value that West might have is the ten of diamonds.

The lead of ◇3 indicates a four or five-card suit, placing South with at least Q-x-x in diamonds. East can work out that if the king of diamonds is played, the contract will be bound to succeed, for there will be no entry to the West hand.

However, if East plays the jack of diamonds, South will almost surely win with the queen (if South does play low, hold your cards back or learn not to trance for half an hour at trick one). After taking the queen of diamonds South will play a heart or a club. East must win at once and play the *king* of diamonds to dummy's ace. On regaining the lead with the other ace (again taking it at once), East will play the third diamond to give West three tricks in the suit.

Note that East must take each ace at the first opportunity (even ducking just once allows declarer to succeed). Likewise the king of diamonds must be sacrificed under the ace. If South began with Q-10-x in diamonds, there was never any defence.

11

Teams. dealer North.
North-South vulnerable.

	♠	A J 4
	♡	Q 6 3
	◇	A 8 2
	♣	A K Q 4

WEST	NORTH	EAST	SOUTH
	2NT	No	3♡
No	4♡	No	4NT*
No	5♠	No	6♡
No	No	No	

*Simple Blackwood

	♠	6 3
	♡	A K J 9 8
	◇	K J 9 4 3
	♣	6

The play:

a) 1 West leads the ♣3. **ace wins**
   2 **Heart to the ace,** everybody follows.
      Plan the play. Will it make any difference if trumps are 3-2 or 4-1?

b) 1 West leads the ♠10. **ace wins**
   2 **Heart to the ace,** everybody follows.
      Plan the play. Will it make any difference if trumps are 3-2 or 4-1?

12

	♠	Q 8 6 4
	♡	10 5 2
	◇	K J 10
	♣	Q J 7

Pairs. dealer West.
North-South vulnerable.

	♠	K J 5
	♡	Q 8 7 4 3
	◇	9 8
	♣	A 8 4

WEST	NORTH	EAST	SOUTH
No	No	No	1NT*
No	3NT	All pass	

*16-18

The play:

1 West leads the ♡4: two. jack. **ace**
2 South leads the ♣3: four. **queen,** five
3 The ♣J is led from dummy: *East discards the two of diamonds,*
   South plays the two and **West wins the ace.**

How should West continue?

13
Teams, dealer South,
East-West vulnerable.

♠ K Q 6 2
♡ A J
◇ A 7 6 5 2
♣ 8 3

WEST	NORTH	EAST	SOUTH
			1NT
No	2♣	No	2◇
No	3NT	All pass	

♠ A 5 3
♡ 8 4 2
◇ 9 8 4 3
♣ A K J

West leads the ♠7. Plan South's play.

14

♠ K Q
♡ 9 7 5 3
◇ J 9 7 5
♣ J 8 4

Teams, dealer North,
both sides vulnerable.

♠ A 9 6 5
♡ 4 2
◇ 10 8 6
♣ 10 7 3 2

WEST	NORTH	EAST	SOUTH
	No	1♡	2♠
No	No	Dble	No
2NT*	3♠	No	4♠
Dble	No	No	No

*Scramble: 'Partner, you pick the spot.'

The play:
1 West leads the ♡4: three, **ace**, eight
2 East returns the ♡10, **South winning with the king**
3 South plays the ♠4: **ace**, queen, eight.

How should West continue?

11. Better safe than sorry

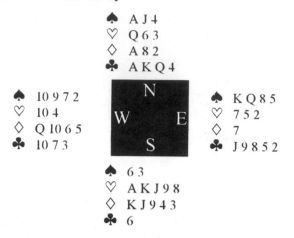

```
                    ♠ A J 4
                    ♡ Q 6 3
                    ◇ A 8 2
                    ♣ A K Q 4

♠ 10 9 7 2              N              ♠ K Q 8 5
♡ 10 4          W            E         ♡ 7 5 2
◇ Q 10 6 5                             ◇ 7
♣ 10 7 3               S               ♣ J 9 8 5 2

                    ♠ 6 3
                    ♡ A K J 9 8
                    ◇ K J 9 4 3
                    ♣ 6
```

The actual declarer failed through careless play. After taking the ace of clubs and drawing trumps, South played a spade to the ace, cashed the top clubs and then played ace and another diamond. On the lie of the cards two diamond tricks now had to be lost.

a) The correct play is to win with the ♣A, draw trumps, then play the ◇K followed by a low diamond towards the A-8, playing the eight if West plays low. This is a standard safety-play which guards against losing more than one diamond trick.

It makes no difference if trumps are 4-1, as long as the diamonds are tackled before taking discards on the clubs and a diamond is not discarded from dummy on the fourth trump.

b) The correct line of play is to take the ♠A, draw trumps, and then play three rounds of clubs, discarding a spade and a diamond, before touching diamonds. If trumps are 3-2, you could continue with the ◇K and a low diamond, as in (a), but if trumps are 4-1, you cannot afford to safety-play the diamonds. If East were to capture the ◇8 on the second round, a black suit return would finish you. You would have to ruff with your last trump and the diamond suit would be blocked.

12. Blockbuster

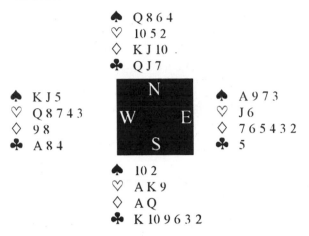

```
              ♠ Q 8 6 4
              ♡ 10 5 2
              ◇ K J 10 .
              ♣ Q J 7
♠ K J 5                          ♠ A 9 7 3
♡ Q 8 7 4 3       N              ♡ J 6
◇ 9 8          W     E           ◇ 7 6 5 4 3 2
♣ A 8 4           S              ♣ 5
              ♠ 10 2
              ♡ A K 9
              ◇ A Q
              ♣ K 10 9 6 3 2
```

West knows from trick one that South began with the A-K-9 of hearts
and from trick three that South began with six clubs. As it is off-beat to
open 1NT with a six-card suit (perhaps less so at match-points), South's
shape will be 2-3-2-6. Likewise West knows that declarer has two heart
tricks and five club tricks. Even without East's ◇ 2, it is clear that there
is no hope of defeating the contract through a diamond switch.

West must switch to spades. leading the jack and playing East to hold
A-x-x-x. with the size of the spot cards being of critical importance. If
East holds A-10-9-x, it would be all right to play the king and then the
jack. The jack first would also work for that holding, and it is the only
card that works on the actual layout.

The ♠5 would block the suit. while the king and then the jack covered
by the queen would leave East on lead at the wrong moment. South has
no answer to the lead of the jack. If the jack is ducked, West continues
with the king and then the five. If the jack is covered by the queen, East
wins with the ace, returns the three to the king, and picks up two more
spade tricks with the 9-7 over dummy's 8-6.

It is also worth noting that with A-K-9 in hand opposite 10-x or 10-x-x
in dummy. declarer should play the ten from dummy. When this is
covered by the jack. the location of the nine is not known. Playing low
marks declarer with the nine when East plays the jack.

13. Keep them guessing

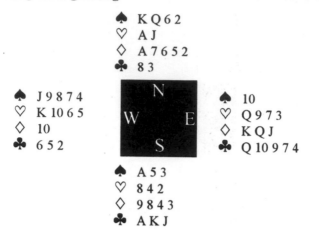

♠ K Q 6 2
♥ A J
♦ A 7 6 5 2
♣ 8 3

♠ J 9 8 7 4
♥ K 10 6 5
♦ 10
♣ 6 5 2

♠ 10
♥ Q 9 7 3
♦ K Q J
♣ Q 10 9 7 4

♠ A 5 3
♥ 8 4 2
♦ 9 8 4 3
♣ A K J

This is merely a matter of setting up some diamond tricks, since you can hardly afford to rely on 3-3 spades and a successful club finesse. But the easier the hand, the easier it can be to overlook a precaution.

The correct play is to win with the king of spades in dummy (no need to tell East that you have the ace) and play a low diamond from both hands. Obviously there will be no problem if the diamonds are 2-2, and if so, it makes no difference whether you play the ace on the first round or the second round.

But if the diamonds are 3-1, the danger is that the defenders may switch to hearts. The advantage of ducking the first round of diamonds is that it gives the defence no chance to signal the heart switch.

At the table the declarer played poorly. After winning the first trick with the ace of spades, South played ace and another diamond. East, with the ten of clubs almost halfway to the table, had a change of mind on seeing partner's discard of the *two* of clubs. A heart was led and the contract went one down.

East might still switch to hearts if left on lead with the first diamond, but you would be unlucky to encounter such a defender. Ninety-nine players out of a hundred would switch to clubs.

14. Show me the way to go

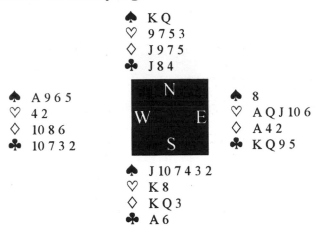

♠ K Q
♥ 9 7 5 3
♦ J 9 7 5
♣ J 8 4

♠ A 9 6 5
♥ 4 2
♦ 10 8 6
♣ 10 7 3 2

♠ 8
♥ A Q J 10 6
♦ A 4 2
♣ K Q 9 5

♠ J 10 7 4 3 2
♥ K 8
♦ K Q 3
♣ A 6

The play to tricks 1 and 2 taken in conjunction with the bidding means that partner began with A-Q-J-10-x in hearts. Partner figures to hold a singleton spade and with a 1-4-4-4, the preferred opening bid is 1 ♦. It follows that partner started with five hearts.

You should take the ten of hearts return as a suit preference signal for a club return: lowest of equals asks for the low suit. Had partner wanted a diamond, the queen of hearts would have been appropriate. With no preference between the minors, partner would have chosen the ♥J.

After the heart lead to the ace, heart return, spade taken by the ace and a club back, the defence can come to five tricks for +500. If you shift to a diamond at trick 4 to East's ace, declarer can unblock an honour and suffer only a one-trick defeat.

After ♦A, East returns a heart, ruffed high by South as West discards a diamond. A spade to the queen and a diamond back to hand allows declarer to play a top spade and concede a spade to West as the last trick for the defence.

15
Dealer North,
both sides vulnerable.

```
            ♠  J 7
            ♡  Q 5 4
            ◇  8 7 6 3 2
            ♣  K Q 4
```

WEST	NORTH	EAST	SOUTH
	No	No	1♠
No	1NT	No	3♠
No	4♠	All pass	

```
            ♠  A K 10 9 4 3
            ♡  8 7 6
            ◇  A
            ♣  A J 5
```

The play:
1 West leads the ♡10: **East wins with the jack**
2 **East cashes the king of hearts,** all follow
3 **East cashes the ace of hearts,** all follow
4 East leads the queen of diamonds, **South wins with the ace.**

How should South continue?

16
Teams, dealer North,
both sides vulnerable.

```
       ♠  A J 7
       ♡  4 3 2
       ◇  K J 5 3
       ♣  J 10 2
```

WEST	NORTH	EAST	SOUTH
	No	No	1♣
No	1◇	No	2NT
No	3NT	All pass	

```
                          ♠  8 4 3 2
                          ♡  Q J 7
                          ◇  9 8 2
                          ♣  A 6 3
```

The play:
1 West leads the ♡6: two, jack, **ace**
2 South leads the ♠10: five, **ace,** four
3 The ♣J is led from dummy . . .

Plan East's defence.

17
Rubber, dealer North,
both sides vulnerable.

	♠	9 6 4 2
	♡	9 8 3 2
	♢	7
	♣	A 10 9 4

WEST	NORTH	EAST	SOUTH
	No	No	2♣
No	2♢	No	2NT
No	3♣*	No	3♢
No	3NT	All pass	

*Stayman

	♠	A K Q
	♡	A K 7
	♢	A Q 10
	♣	Q 6 3 2

The play:
1 West leads the ♢5: seven. jack. **queen.**

Plan South's play.

18

	♠	A K J 10 6 3
	♡	7 5
	♢	K 4
	♣	8 7 6

Pairs, dealer South,
both sides vulnerable.

♠	9
♡	K J 9 4
♢	J 7 6 5 2
♣	A J 5

WEST	NORTH	EAST	SOUTH
			1♣
No	1♠	No	1NT*
No	3♠	No	3NT
No	No	No	

*12-14 points

The play:
1 West leads the ♢5: **king**, ten, three
2 The ♣6 is led from dummy: four, king . . .

How should West defend?

15. It all adds up

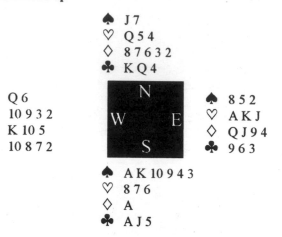

♠ J 7
♡ Q 5 4
◇ 8 7 6 3 2
♣ K Q 4

♠ Q 6
♡ 10 9 3 2
◇ K 10 5
♣ 10 8 7 2

♠ 8 5 2
♡ A K J
◇ Q J 9 4
♣ 9 6 3

♠ A K 10 9 4 3
♡ 8 7 6
◇ A
♣ A J 5

To make the contract South has to avoid losing a trump trick. There is no excuse for going wrong, for all the clues to the right play have been paraded by the defence. East has shown up with eight points in hearts and two points in diamonds. The lead of the queen of diamonds almost certainly implies the jack of diamonds, making a total of eleven points. Having passed originally, East can hardly have the queen of spades, for that would mean thirteen points and an opening bid.

There is no percentage in taking a finesse that is known to be wrong. South should play the ace and king of spades and hope to drop the queen singleton or doubleton in the West hand. East, of course, would be better advised in future not to reveal so much in the early play.

Principle: The right way to play a suit in the abstract may be to finesse, but it is not necessarily the right way to play the whole hand.

16. Second hand rose

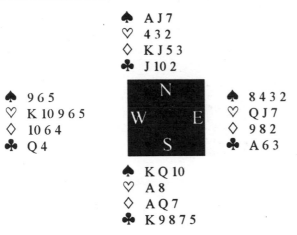

```
                    ♠  A J 7
                    ♡  4 3 2
                    ◇  K J 5 3
                    ♣  J 10 2

    ♠  9 6 5              N              ♠  8 4 3 2
    ♡  K 10 9 6 5    W        E          ♡  Q J 7
    ◇  10 6 4                            ◇  9 8 2
    ♣  Q 4               S              ♣  A 6 3

                    ♠  K Q 10
                    ♡  A 8
                    ◇  A Q 7
                    ♣  K 9 8 7 5
```

East must rise with the ace of clubs and continue hearts to defeat the contract by one trick. If East plays low, South goes up with the king and runs for home with nine tricks.

How can East tell what to do? Well, if the six of hearts is a normal fourth-highest lead, East can be certain that partner has the king of hearts. From the rule of eleven, East knows that South began with two hearts higher than the six. If these are the ace and king, West must have started with 10-9-8-6(-5), but that is not possible since West would have led the ten from such a holding. Very often *reductio ad absurdum* arguments can point the right way.

South knew, of course, that it was pointless to hold up the ace as the lead of the six of hearts could not be from a six-card suit.

East has a further safeguard. If South really intended to let the jack of clubs run for a finesse, the finesse will probably be repeated later, as a defender will often rise with the ace when holding A-Q-x

33

17. The whole is greater than the sum of the parts

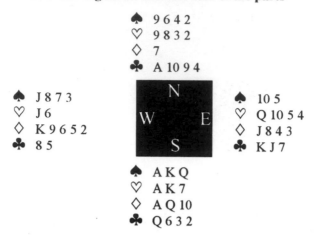

```
              ♠  9 6 4 2
              ♡  9 8 3 2
              ◇  7
              ♣  A 10 9 4
  ♠  J 8 7 3        N        ♠  10 5
  ♡  J 6                     ♡  Q 10 5 4
  ◇  K 9 6 5 2  W       E    ◇  J 8 4 3
  ♣  8 5             S       ♣  K J 7
              ♠  A K Q
              ♡  A K 7
              ◇  A Q 10
              ♣  Q 6 3 2
```

The best method of playing a suit does not necessarily correspond with
the correct way of playing a hand. That's why the mathematician, who
knows the best mathematical play in a suit, is not always a strong bridge
player. The problems of a whole hand only rarely reduce to the proper
handling of a single suit.

Here South needs to establish a second club trick to make the contract.
In theory the correct way of handling the club holding is to take two
finesses, but that would be the only way to go down on the given hand.
The safety of the contract requires that East be kept off lead, so that a
second diamond lead does not come through the A-10 until the extra
club trick has been established. If a club finesse is taken into the East
hand, the diamond return punctures South's tenace and the contract fails
('Unlucky, partner, both clubs were wrong. . .').

Since West is not dangerous on lead, the correct play is a club to the ace
and a club back, playing the queen if East follows low. Even if both
honours are with West, or if West has K-x and East J-x-x, the contract is
safe, for South establishes the ninth trick in clubs before the defenders
can get the diamonds going.

18. Chime time

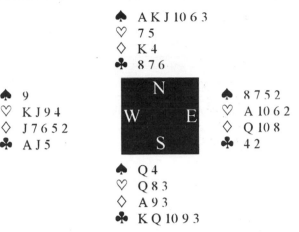

Spades: A K J 10 6 3
Hearts: 7 5
Diamonds: K 4
Clubs: 8 7 6

West:
Spades: 9
Hearts: K J 9 4
Diamonds: J 7 6 5 2
Clubs: A J 5

East:
Spades: 8 7 5 2
Hearts: A 10 6 2
Diamonds: Q 10 8
Clubs: 4 2

South:
Spades: Q 4
Hearts: Q 8 3
Diamonds: A 9 3
Clubs: K Q 10 9 3

West should take the ace of clubs and switch to the four of hearts. If West ducks the king of clubs or takes the ace but continues diamonds, the declarer makes nine fast tricks.

West should have heard the alarm bells ringing when South won the diamond lead in dummy and played clubs, not spades. For this play to make any sense, the declarer must have the queen of spades. Otherwise South would win the diamond lead in hand with the ace and attack spades, retaining the king of diamonds in dummy as an entry for the established spades.

With the queen of spades, South can be counted for eight tricks (six spades and two diamonds), and almost certainly the queen of clubs along with the king. That means the contract is home if South regains the lead quickly.

All the evidence indicates the need for an urgent heart switch, but many defenders would mechanically continue diamonds, reassured by East's ten of diamonds at trick one. East must encourage diamonds, of course, since West may have the ace.

19

Teams, dealer West,
neither side vulnerable.

	♠	7 3 2
	♡	8 7 4 3 2
	◇	K Q
	♣	9 5 2

WEST	NORTH	EAST	SOUTH
No	No	No	2♣
No	2◇	No	3♣
No	4♣	No	6♣
No	No	No	

	♠	A 6 4
	♡	A
	◇	A J 5
	♣	A K J 8 7 4

The play:
1 West leads the ♡K: two, five, **ace**
2 **South plays the ♣A:** six, two, queen.

How should South continue?

20

	♠	A J
	♡	K Q 8 6
	◇	3
	♣	A K 8 4 3 2

Teams, dealer East,
both sides vulnerable.

	♠	Q 10 5 2
	♡	9 2
	◇	A 8 7
	♣	Q J 6 5

WEST	NORTH	EAST	SOUTH
		5◇	No
No	Dble	No	5♡
No	No	No	

The play:
1 **West leads the ◇A:** three, four, two

What should West play at trick 2?

21
Teams, dealer East,
both sides vulnerable.

♠ J
♡ K
♢ J 7 4 3 2
♣ A K 9 8 4 2

WEST	NORTH	EAST	SOUTH
		No	1♠
No	2♣	No	2♠
No	3♢	No	3NT
No	No	No	

♠ A 6 4 3 2
♡ A 9 8
♢ A 8
♣ 10 6 3

The play:
1 West leads the ♡5: **king**, six, eight

How should declarer continue?

22
Teams, dealer East,
North-South vulnerable.

♠ Q J 10 7 4
♡ A
♢ 7 6 5 3 2
♣ Q 5

WEST	NORTH	EAST	SOUTH
		No	1♡
No	1♠	No	2NT*
No	3♠	No	3NT
No	No	No	

♠ A 9 8 6 3
♡ 7 6 5
♢ K 9
♣ 10 6 4

*Natural, 19-20 points, game-force

The play:
1 West leads the ♣7: **queen**, six, two
2 The ♠4 is led from dummy . . .

Plan East's defence

19. From tyro to maestro

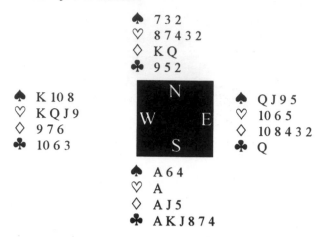

```
                    ♠ 7 3 2
                    ♡ 8 7 4 3 2
                    ◇ K Q
                    ♣ 9 5 2
   ♠ K 10 8                      ♠ Q J 9 5
   ♡ K Q J 9      N              ♡ 10 6 5
   ◇ 9 7 6     W     E           ◇ 10 8 4 3 2
   ♣ 10 6 3       S              ♣ Q
                    ♠ A 6 4
                    ♡ A
                    ◇ A J 5
                    ♣ A K J 8 7 4
```

The fall of the queen of clubs simplifies the problem, but the best line applies whether the queen appears or not.

The novice draws three rounds of trumps. Result : two spade losers.

The moderate player draws a second round of trumps ('just to check that the queen was singleton, partner'), then plays three rounds of diamonds to discard a spade from dummy. Next comes ace and another spade, but West wins and plays a third round of trumps, leaving South with a second spade loser.

The competent player does not draw a second round of trumps, but plays three rounds of diamonds, pitching the spade from dummy, then ace and another spade, eventually ruffing the third spade in dummy.

The expert plays a low spade from both hands at trick three. On winning the return, discard dummy's second spade on the third diamond, cash the ace of spades, ruff the third spade and draw the outstanding trumps.

Why does the expert adopt this line? Because the approach of the competent player attracts an unnecessary risk. After three rounds of diamonds and ace and another spade, East can win and play a fourth diamond, promoting a trump trick for West. There is no such risk attached to the expert's line.

Well, which category did you achieve?

20. No crystal ball needed

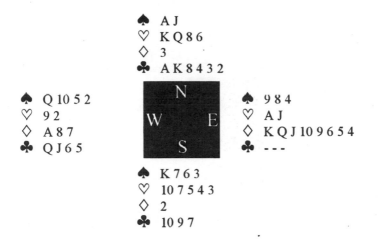

```
              ♠ A J
              ♡ K Q 8 6
              ◇ 3
              ♣ A K 8 4 3 2
                    N
♠ Q 10 5 2                        ♠ 9 8 4
♡ 9 2          W        E         ♡ A J
◇ A 8 7                           ◇ K Q J 10 9 6 5 4
♣ Q J 6 5           S             ♣ - - -
              ♠ K 7 6 3
              ♡ 10 7 5 4 3
              ◇ 2
              ♣ 10 9 7
```

South would have been well-advised to pass North's double but South
will feel joy, not remorse, if 5♡ makes. A club at trick 2 ensures defeat
and you do not need a crystal ball to find that switch. Partner's ◇4 on
your lead should be clear-cut as a suit-preference signal for a club:
lowest card asks for the low suit. While it is usually not best to attack
dummy's long suit, that counts for nothing if partner's signal is
unmistakable. When a continuation of the suit you have led is out of the
question, partner's card should be taken as a suit-preference signal.

If you switch to a spade at trick 2, the contract can be made, particularly
if declarer reads East's ◇4 better than you have. South would win with
dummy's jack and play the ♡K taken by the ace. The spade return
would be won by the ace followed by the queen of hearts, drawing
trumps, and the ♡6, overtaken by the ♡7.

South would then lead the ♣10 or ♣9, running it if West plays low. If
West covers the club, dummy wins, the ♡8 is overtaken by the ♡10
and the club finesse will then see declarer home.

In an experienced partnership, East might well double 5♡ (analogous to
a Lightner double of a slam) to ask for an unusual lead. That would also
put partner on the right track after the ◇A holds.

21. Category mistake

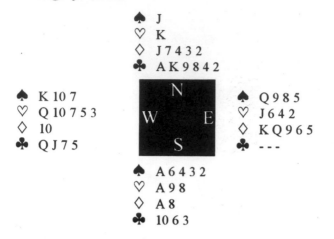

```
              ♠  J
              ♡  K
              ◇  J 7 4 3 2
              ♣  A K 9 8 4 2

♠  K 10 7              N              ♠  Q 9 8 5
♡  Q 10 7 5 3      W       E          ♡  J 6 4 2
◇  10                  S              ◇  K Q 9 6 5
♣  Q J 7 5                            ♣  - - -

              ♠  A 6 4 3 2
              ♡  A 9 8
              ◇  A 8
              ♣  10 6 3
```

The poor player continues with the ace and king of clubs, and even if the ten of clubs is unblocked, 3NT will succeed only 40% of the time. The contract will fail on this line whenever the clubs are 3-1 or 4-0.

The average player wins with the king of hearts and then plays the ace of clubs followed by a low club. This caters for any 2-2 or 3-1 break, but if the hand is as shown above, this play will fail. West should play low on the second round of clubs and the declarer will be left with only three club tricks.

Through bitter experience, the top player knows that the right play after winning the king of hearts is to lead a low club from dummy at once. This is a 95% play, succeeding in every position except when East has all four clubs. If West ducks the ten of clubs on the above layout, declarer can make an overtrick by taking the double club finesse.

22. Rise and shine

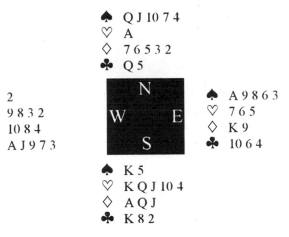

```
              ♠ Q J 10 7 4
              ♡ A
              ◇ 7 6 5 3 2
              ♣ Q 5
♠ 2                              ♠ A 9 8 6 3
♡ 9 8 3 2          N             ♡ 7 6 5
◇ 10 8 4       W       E         ◇ K 9
♣ A J 9 7 3        S             ♣ 10 6 4
              ♠ K 5
              ♡ K Q J 10 4
              ◇ A Q J
              ♣ K 8 2
```

East should rise with the ace of spades and return a club, setting the contract by one trick.

In view of South's strong rebid and the strength in dummy, the defence cannot hope to prevail by the passive approach of ducking the first spade and thus limiting declarer to three spade tricks. Unless the clubs can be run, it is unlikely that the defence can come to five tricks.

The deal arose between the U.S. Aces and France in the 1971 Bermuda Bowl. Bobby Wolff, East, correctly rose with the ace of spades and · returned a club to defeat three no-trumps. The same contract was made in the other room when the declarer took the diamond finesse at trick two, making five heart tricks, three diamonds and a club.

There is not much to choose between the lines adopted by the two declarers, each depending essentially on a key honour being well-placed. Playing on the spades has a slight advantage by capitalizing on a possible 4-4 break in clubs.

Note that if East ducks the first spade, the declarer is hardly likely to play a second spade and allow East a chance to recover from the error. Declarer will cross to the ace of hearts, take the diamond finesse and make the contract that way (with an overtrick as it happens).

23
Teams. dealer South.
North-South vulnerable.

♠ A K 7
♡ A J 8 3
◇ Q 7 4 2
♣ A 6

WEST	NORTH	EAST	SOUTH
			1♡
1♠	2♣	No	2NT
No	4NT (1)	No	5♠ (2)
No	6♡	All pass	

(1) Roman Key Card Blackwood
based on hearts
(2) 2 key cards + the ♡Q

♠ J 6 4 2
♡ K Q 7 6
◇ A J
♣ K J 9

The play:
1 West leads the ♡5: three. ten, **king**
2 South plays ♡6: four, **ace,** two
3 Dummy plays ♡8: *East discards ◇6,* **queen**, nine
How should South continue?

24
Rubber. dealer South.
North-South vulnerable.

♠ A 9 8 5 2
♡ 10 6
◇ A 9
♣ 10 6 5 3

WEST	NORTH	EAST	SOUTH
			1♡*
4◇	4♡**	All pass	

*5+ suit
**Succumbing to pressure

♠ J 7 3
♡ Q J 9 4
◇ Q 3
♣ 9 7 4 2

The play:
1 West leads the ♣J: three. two. **ace**
2-3 **South cashes the ♡A, ♡K:** West follows with the three and eight
4 South plays the ♡2: *West discards the ◇8,* declarer looks annoyed.
a spade is pitched from dummy and **East wins with the jack of hearts.**
5 **East leads ◇Q:** four, two, nine

How should East continue?

25
Teams, dealer West,
neither side vulnerable.

♠ A K 5 3
♡ 7 3 2
◇ A K Q 5
♣ Q 4

WEST	NORTH	EAST	SOUTH
3♣	Double*	No	4♡
No	No	No	

♠ J 4
♡ A K 10 8 4
◇ J 10 7 2
♣ 6 3

The play :
1 West leads the ◇3: **ace,** four, two
2 ♡2 from dummy: five, **ace,** jack

How should South continue?

26
Teams, dealer South,
both sides vulnerable.

♠ 7 6 3
♡ Q 8
◇ A K Q 8 7 3
♣ Q 8

WEST	NORTH	EAST	SOUTH
			1♠
No	2◇	No	2♠
No	4♠	All pass	

♠ 9 4 2
♡ K 6
◇ J 6 5
♣ A J 5 4 2

The play:
1 West leads the ♣6 . . .

Plan the defence for East.

23. Backward finesse or no finesse?

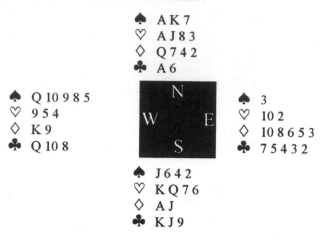

```
                    ♠  A K 7
                    ♡  A J 8 3
                    ◇  Q 7 4 2
                    ♣  A 6
♠  Q 10 9 8 5                              ♠  3
♡  9 5 4            N                      ♡  10 2
◇  K 9         W        E                  ◇  10 8 6 5 3
♣  Q 10 8           S                      ♣  7 5 4 3 2
                    ♠  J 6 4 2
                    ♡  K Q 7 6
                    ◇  A J
                    ♣  K J 9
```

Given West's overcall, it is highly likely that West holds all the missing picture cards. Assuming that there will be a diamond loser, you need to discard two spades from your hand or one spade from dummy.

If you can create a third winner in clubs, that will provide a parking spot for dummy's spade loser. One idea, assuming West holds the ♣Q, is to lead the ♣J from hand and if covered, capture the queen with the ace and follow with a finesse of the ♣9. This succeeds if West has the ♣Q and East the ♣10. You could try the diamond finesse and if that fails, fall back on the backward club finesse.

However, if you are confident that West does hold the missing high cards, you have a better play available. Cash the ace of spades (just in case West has been frivolous and East has the ♠Q bare) and continue with a diamond to the ace and then the jack of diamonds.

West presumably started with five spades and has shown up with three hearts. If holding the ◇K doubleton, West will be endplayed on winning with the ◇K. You will run a spade exit to your jack while a club exit gives you the desired third trick there. If West exits with a diamond, you win with the queen and will have to decide whether to play East for six clubs to the queen (cash ♣A and finesse ♣J) or play West for ♣Q-x (cash ♣A and ♣K). If West is a sound bidder, the latter is the better bet.

24. Don't hang on . . . for dear life

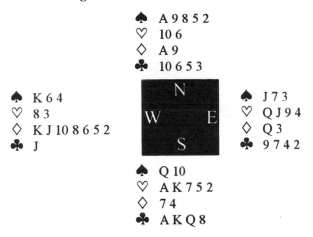

```
              ♠ A 9 8 5 2
              ♡ 10 6
              ◇ A 9
              ♣ 10 6 5 3

♠ K 6 4          N          ♠ J 7 3
♡ 8 3                       ♡ Q J 9 4
◇ K J 10 8 6 5 2  W   E     ◇ Q 3
♣ J              S          ♣ 9 7 4 2

              ♠ Q 10
              ♡ A K 7 5 2
              ◇ 7 4
              ♣ A K Q 8
```

When the queen of diamonds is allowed to hold, you must cash your top trump before continuing with a second diamond. You should assume West's jack of clubs lead to be a singleton (few competent players lead from J-x unless partner has bid the suit). South then can be assumed to have started with five hearts, four clubs, two diamonds (why else duck the diamond?) and hence two spades (without the king if you are to have any chance).

If you fail to cash your top heart but play another diamond, declarer will take the ace, play off the clubs and then throw you in with the heart. You will have to lead a spade and if South guesses right, inserting the ten, the contract will make. Indeed, South should guess right, for if you held the king of spades, West should have overtaken the queen of diamonds in order to play a spade.

Why did South look annoyed? Because the realization came, a second too late, that a better chance had been missed. After two rounds of hearts, it is better to switch to the double spade finesse to eliminate the diamond loser. The hearts were unlikely to split 3-3 on the bidding.

South will be even more annoyed when North points out (as partners always do) that a second opportunity was missed. If South wins the first diamond, cashes the clubs and plays another diamond, the defence cannot avoid eliminating South's spade loser in the end-game.

25. Believe only half of what you see

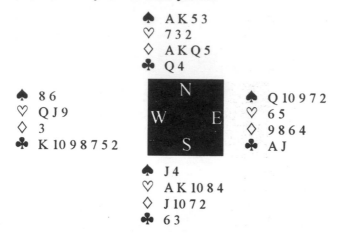

```
                    ♠  A K 5 3
                    ♡  7 3 2
                    ◇  A K Q 5
                    ♣  Q 4
    ♠  8 6                              ♠  Q 10 9 7 2
    ♡  Q J 9                            ♡  6 5
    ◇  3                                ◇  9 8 6 4
    ♣  K 10 9 8 7 5 2                   ♣  A J
                    ♠  J 4
                    ♡  A K 10 8 4
                    ◇  J 10 7 2
                    ♣  6 3
```

When you saw the three of diamonds, no doubt the thought crossed your mind, 'Probably a singleton lead'. When a pre-emptor leads some suit other than the one he bid, a singleton is a popular choice.

When you led a trump to the ace and West produced the jack of hearts, again your little grey cells would have flashed a message, 'Could easily be a singleton'. It is not likely that West has a singleton in both red suits and so the question is, which singleton should you believe?

The good news is that you have a safe continuation by playing off the king of hearts. When the trumps divide 3-2 as above, you lose just one trump and two clubs. If West did start with ♡J singleton and East with ♡Q-9-6-5, you cross to dummy with a spade and lead dummy's third trump to hold East to just one trump trick.

The danger is to pay too much attention to the jack of hearts and the theory of restricted choice. If you cross to dummy at trick three and lead a trump to your ten (or eight), West wins, plays a club to East and receives a diamond ruff. The king of clubs is the fourth trick for the defence. The safe way to play the trump suit may not be the safest way to play the complete hand.

26. Just deserts

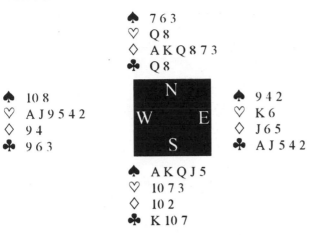

```
              ♠  7 6 3
              ♡  Q 8
              ◇  A K Q 8 7 3
              ♣  Q 8

♠  10 8                        ♠  9 4 2
♡  A J 9 5 4 2                 ♡  K 6
◇  9 4         W        E      ◇  J 6 5
♣  9 6 3                       ♣  A J 5 4 2

              ♠  A K Q J 5
              ♡  10 7 3
              ◇  10 2
              ♣  K 10 7
```

Firstly, when dummy plays low, do not play the jack. It can be right to finesse against dummy but not here. If partner has the king of clubs, playing the ace will not hurt. If partner does not have the king, playing the ace is essential. When dummy has a long, strong suit to provide discards for declarer, you have to collect your tricks quickly or not at all. If the cards are as above and you play the ♣J, declarer makes twelve tricks and the other three players (plus any kibitzers) make a mental note to erase your telephone number from their list of potential partners.

Having taken the ace of clubs, what next? Returning partner's suit can be a sensible move but always check first how many tricks that might give you. You need four tricks to defeat declarer but a club return can score one more trick at best. Where are the other two tricks?

Count the visible high card points. Dummy has 13, you have 9. That makes 22. Give declarer 12 or so for opening the bidding and partner can have 6 at best. If partner does have the ♣K, you have virtually no chance to beat this game.

The best hope is to play partner for the ace of hearts. Take the ace of clubs and switch to the ♡K. When that wins, a heart to the ace and a heart ruff bring you the deserved reward.

The switch to the ♡K can hardly cost. If declarer has the ♡A, declarer would discard any heart losers on dummy's diamonds anyway.

PART 2: Intermediate Level

27
Rubber, dealer East,
East-West vulnerable.

♠ 8 3 2
♡ Q 6
◇ 9 8 6 4
♣ A K J 9

WEST	NORTH	EAST	SOUTH
		No	1♠
No	2♣	No	3♣
No	3♠	No	4♠
No	No	No	

N W E S

♠ A 7 6 5 4
♡ A 5 3
◇ A
♣ Q 8 6 4

The play:
1 West leads the ♠K: two, nine . . .

Plan South's play.

28
Rubber, dealer South,
neither side vulnerable.

♠ Q 8 7
♡ 7 5 4
◇ J 8 7 2
♣ Q 9 3

WEST	NORTH	EAST	SOUTH
			2NT*
No	3NT	All pass	

*21-22 points

N W E S

♠ K 9 5
♡ A Q J 6
◇ 9 5 4
♣ 8 6 2

The play:
1 West leads the ♠J: seven, five, **ace**
2 South leads the ◇Q: **king,** two, four
3 West leads the ♠10: queen, **king,** two.

How should East continue?

29
Dealer East,
both sides vulnerable.

♠ Q 6 5
♡ 6 4
♢ A Q 6 5 3
♣ A 4 3

WEST	NORTH	EAST	SOUTH
		No	1NT
No	3NT	All pass	

♠ A K J 10
♡ A 5 2
♢ 7 4 2
♣ J 8 7

The play:
1 West leads the ♡3, East plays the king.

How should South play?

30
Dealer North,
East-West vulnerable.

♠ 6
♡ K 8 3
♢ A K 10 9 8 5 3
♣ Q 4

WEST	NORTH	EAST	SOUTH
	1♢	No	1♠
2♡	3♢	No	6♠
No	No	No	

♠ 9 5 4
♡ J 7 6
♢ Q 7 4 2
♣ K 7 2

The play:
1 West leads the ♣5: queen, king, **ace**
2 **South plays the ♠A**: seven, six, five
3 **South plays the ♠K**: queen, *dummy discards ♡3, ♠4*
4 **South plays the ♠J**: *West discards ♡10, dummy throws ♢3*
5 South leads the ♢J: *West discards ♡2, dummy plays low . . .*

How should East defend?

27. Ask little, receive much

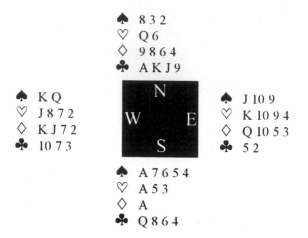

```
              ♠ 8 3 2
              ♡ Q 6
              ◇ 9 8 6 4
              ♣ A K J 9
♠ K Q                        ♠ J 10 9
♡ J 8 7 2         N          ♡ K 10 9 4
◇ K J 7 2     W       E      ◇ Q 10 5 3
♣ 10 7 3          S          ♣ 5 2
              ♠ A 7 6 5 4
              ♡ A 5 3
              ◇ A
              ♣ Q 8 6 4
```

The novice wins the first spade, succeeding if West holds the ♡K, but failing in most layouts when the king of hearts is wrong since the defenders will usually clear trumps. Winning the first spade succeeds on the actual deal above but only because the trumps are blocked.

The good player ducks the first spade, wins the second and leads a heart. This will succeed if West has the king of hearts or if East has the king but not the last trump. This line will make four spades most of the time but not on the actual deal.

The expert succeeds whenever trumps are 3-2 regardless of the location of the king of hearts. After winning the second spade, continue with the ace of diamonds, a club to the ace, ruff a diamond, play a club to the king, ruff a diamond, play a club to the jack and ruff a diamond. If a defender ruffs at any time, dummy has a trump left to take care of declarer's last heart. If the master trump is still at large, South continues with the queen of clubs. If this is ruffed, declarer still makes the ace of hearts and a heart ruff (on the actual deal, East would give declarer eleven tricks if the queen of clubs is ruffed as East has to lead away from the king of hearts). If the queen of clubs is not ruffed, declarer just cashes the ace of hearts for the tenth trick.

28. Hold your horses

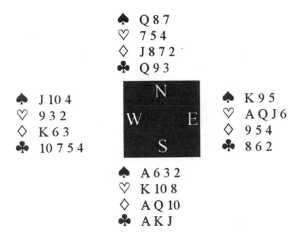

♠ Q 8 7
♡ 7 5 4
◇ J 8 7 2
♣ Q 9 3

♠ J 10 4
♡ 9 3 2
◇ K 6 3
♣ 10 7 5 4

♠ K 9 5
♡ A Q J 6
◇ 9 5 4
♣ 8 6 2

♠ A 6 3 2
♡ K 10 8
◇ A Q 10
♣ A K J

East must switch at once to hearts in order to establish a fifth trick for the defence.

At the table East cashed the nine of spades and then led the queen of hearts. The declarer played the king and had nine tricks by virtue of the thirteenth spade.

Once West has shown up with the jack of spades and the king of diamonds South is marked with all the remaining high cards because of the 2NT opening. East should realize that West has led from a short suit. From J-10-x-x fourth highest would be normal, while the jack lead is consistent with J-10-9-x or J-10-8-x (neither of which is possible here) or with J-10-x. Once East appreciates that West has made a short suit lead, East will not be tempted to cash the nine of spades as that can help only declarer.

The heart switch is needed to set up an additional heart winner while the spade control is still held. If declarer is able to run for home with one spade, one heart, three diamonds and four clubs, there was nothing you could have done.

29. A psychological edge

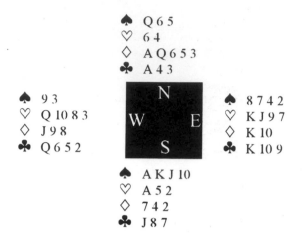

♠ Q 6 5
♡ 6 4
◇ A Q 6 5 3
♣ A 4 3

♠ 9 3
♡ Q 10 8 3
◇ J 9 8
♣ Q 6 5 2

♠ 8 7 4 2
♡ K J 9 7
◇ K 10
♣ K 10 9

♠ A K J 10
♡ A 5 2
◇ 7 4 2
♣ J 8 7

In practice declarer failed. The ace of hearts was held up until the third round. Declarer then led a diamond to the queen and king.

The correct play at trick one is the ace of hearts. The opening lead is likely to be an honest fourth-highest, and as you can see the *two* of hearts, the lead of the *three* means that the hearts are 4-4. It would be unfortunate (partner is sure to have a stronger word for it) if you ducked the heart and East returned a club in a situation where the contract could have been made by taking the ace of hearts and tackling the diamonds.

To make 3NT you will need to bring in the diamond suit. The 'natural' play is to finesse the queen, but on the given layout this fails. Why not try a psychological approach which does nothing to jeopardize your chances? Cross to the queen of spades and lead a low diamond from dummy. East may well think that you have the jack and go up with the king, ending your problems. Your play is a neat variation of the principle— *If you have to lose a trick to set up a long suit, lose it early.*

If East plays low smoothly you can take the normal finesse of the queen later. The first-round finesse works 50% of the time. The delayed finesse also works 50% of the time plus the occasions when East with K-x or even K-x-x goes wrong. It is a something-for-nothing play.

30. Accepting Greek gifts

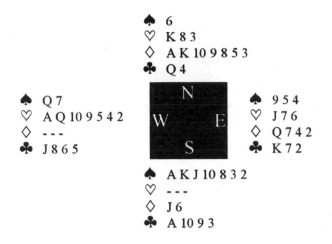

♠ 6
♡ K 8 3
◇ A K 10 9 8 5 3
♣ Q 4

♠ Q 7
♡ A Q 10 9 5 4 2
◇ - - -
♣ J 8 6 5

♠ 9 5 4
♡ J 7 6
◇ Q 7 4 2
♣ K 7 2

♠ A K J 10 8 3 2
♡ - - -
◇ J 6
♣ A 10 9 3

East should take the queen of diamonds at once and return a club.

How can East tell to return a club and not a heart? Well, it helps to
know the calibre of the opposition, of course, but surely no sane South
would have jumped to six spades missing the queen of trumps, the top
diamonds and the king and queen of clubs if there was a heart loser as
well. There is, after all, a convention known as Blackwood.

In general, it is good advice to beware of Greek gifts, and many players
would duck the first diamond in order to shut out dummy's suit. But in
this case the declarer does not need more than three tricks from the
diamonds. If East ducks, South continues with the ace and king of
diamonds, pitching a club, and then concedes a club to the jack. East's
duck gives South the chance to recover from the wrong guess at trick
one as well as a story to tell (at your expense) for weeks to come.

East should realize that the fate of the slam depends on the location of
the jack of clubs. If South has it, twelve tricks are bound to be there
whether the first diamond is ducked or not.

31
Dealer North,
neither side vulnerable.

♠ 10 6 2
♡ 9 8 7 3
♢ K 5
♣ A J 6 2

WEST	NORTH	EAST	SOUTH
	No	No	1♡
No	2♡	2♠	3♡
No	No	No	

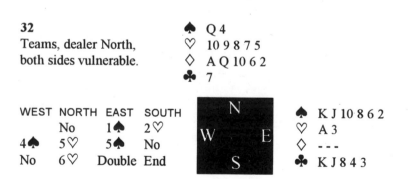

♠ Q 7
♡ A K J 10 6
♢ Q 10 3
♣ Q 5 4

The play:
1 West leads the ♠5: two, **king,** seven
2 **East cashes ♠A:** queen, eight, six
3 East leads ♡5: **ace,** four, three
4 South plays ♢3 to the **king,** which wins.

How should South continue?

32
Teams, dealer North,
both sides vulnerable.

♠ Q 4
♡ 10 9 8 7 5
♢ A Q 10 6 2
♣ 7

WEST	NORTH	EAST	SOUTH
	No	1♠	2♡
4♠	5♡	5♠	No
No	6♡	Double	End

♠ K J 10 8 6 2
♡ A 3
♢ - - -
♣ K J 8 4 3

West leads the ace of spades. Plan East's defence.

33
Rubber, dealer West,
neither side vulnerable.

♠ K 10 9 5 2
♡ K 4
◇ 10 7 6 4 2
♣ 5

WEST	NORTH	EAST	SOUTH
3♣	No	No	3♡
No	4♡	All pass	

♠ A 7 3
♡ A Q J 9 6 5
◇ 3
♣ J 10 3

The play:

1 **West leads ♣K:** five, two, three
2 West switches to ♡3.

Plan South's play.

34
Rubber, dealer North,
neither side vulnerable.

♠ 2
♡ A Q 7 5 3
◇ K 8 5
♣ A K J 3

WEST	NORTH	EAST	SOUTH
	1♡	2◇	2♠
No	3♣	No	3♠
No	3NT	No	4♠
No	No	No	

♠ A 3
♡ K 10 9 8
◇ Q J 9 7 6 2
♣ 9

The play:

1 **West leads ◇A:** five, queen, four
2 West leads ◇3: **king,** two, ten
3 The ♠2 is led from dummy . . .

How should East defend?

31. All in good time

```
            ♠ 10 6 2
            ♡ 9 8 7 3
            ◇ K 5
            ♣ A J 6 2

♠ 8 5 4              N              ♠ A K J 9 3
♡ Q 4 2         W        E         ♡ 5
◇ A 9 7                            ◇ J 8 6 4 2
♣ K 9 8 3            S             ♣ 10 7

            ♠ Q 7
            ♡ A K J 10 6
            ◇ Q 10 3
            ♣ Q 5 4
```

Declarer failed in practice by playing a trump from dummy at trick five. After winning with the king of hearts, South took the club finesse, followed by a diamond to the ten and ace. West simply cashed the queen of hearts and exited with a spade (a diamond would have done as well), leaving South with a club loser for one down.

Declarer mistimed the play. If the hearts are 2-2, there is no urgency about drawing the second round. Best at trick five is to return a diamond to the ten and ace. South can ruff the spade return, lead a low club to the jack, a heart to the king, then cash the queen of diamonds and throw West in with the heart to lead away from the king of clubs.

It would not matter if West held an extra diamond or spade instead of the fourth club. It would then be a choice of poisons: lead away from the king of clubs or give South a ruff and discard.

South can also succeed if West has the jack of diamonds as well as the ace, provided that West has no more than three cards in both spades and diamonds.

32. Sledgehammer produces cracking results

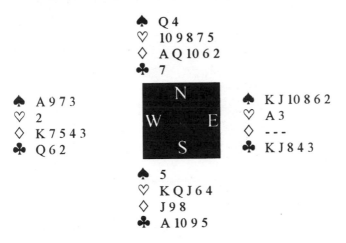

```
              ♠  Q 4
              ♡  10 9 8 7 5
              ◇  A Q 10 6 2
              ♣  7

♠ A 9 7 3            N            ♠ K J 10 8 6 2
♡ 2                               ♡ A 3
◇ K 7 5 4 3    W         E        ◇ - - -
♣ Q 6 2                           ♣ K J 8 4 3
                     S

              ♠  5
              ♡  K Q J 6 4
              ◇  J 9 8
              ♣  A 10 9 5
```

Six spades goes down only if North-South find the club ruff, but that does not mean you should settle for less than the maximum penalty. Obviously you want partner to give you a diamond ruff, but how can you focus attention on the diamonds? A high spade would merely request a spade continuation. Some partnerships play that a high spot card asks for a continuation, while an honour indicates suit preference, but for most partnerships the jack of spades would be a command to continue spades. A low spade would ask for a switch, but would partner find the right switch? There's a rhetorical question if ever there was one.

At the table East played the *two* of spades at trick one. West, staring at the king of diamonds, reasoned that East was unlikely to want a diamond shift. The club switch allowed declarer to escape for one down.

The dramatic card, and the right card to play at trick one, is the *king* — an impossible card in any natural sense. If partner now doesn't work out that a diamond switch is required, it's time to invest in a new partner.

Isn't it dangerous to play the king of spades? If declarer ruffs the first trick you will have set up the queen of spades as a winner. Even so, it is unlikely that the queen of spades will provide South with a useful discard. Any missing diamond honours are onside, and South can hardly hold a singleton club loser.

33. Duck for dinner

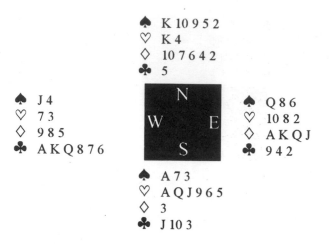

```
                    ♠  K 10 9 5 2
                    ♡  K 4
                    ◊  10 7 6 4 2
                    ♣  5

♠  J 4                                   ♠  Q 8 6
♡  7 3              N                    ♡  10 8 2
◊  9 8 5        W       E                ◊  A K Q J
♣  A K Q 8 7 6      S                    ♣  9 4 2

                    ♠  A 7 3
                    ♡  A Q J 9 6 5
                    ◊  3
                    ♣  J 10 3
```

But for that annoying trump switch you might have been able to ruff both remaining club losers in dummy.

The worst way of tackling the hand would be to draw the rest of the trumps immediately. You would then succeed only on some miraculous spade position, for if you lost a spade the opponents could cash a diamond and two more clubs for two down.

A slight improvement would be to ruff a club in dummy, return to the ace of spades, draw trumps and then duck a spade. That could work if East won the spade and had no more clubs and West had no quick entry in diamonds, or if the defenders tried to cash diamonds instead of clubs.

But the best chance is to bank on 3-2 spades and duck a spade at trick three. No matter in which hand that trick is won, the defenders are helpless. As soon as you regain the lead you can draw trumps and run the spades for ten tricks. The key is to leave the second trump in dummy to control the club suit while you go about establishing the spades.

If the spades turn out to be 4-1 and someone scores a ruff, console yourself with the thought that you could not make the contract anyway.

34. Fools rush in

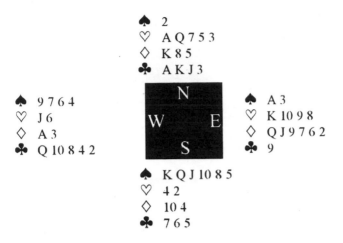

```
              ♠  2
              ♡  A Q 7 5 3
              ◇  K 8 5
              ♣  A K J 3

♠  9 7 6 4         N          ♠  A 3
♡  J 6                        ♡  K 10 9 8
◇  A 3       W         E      ◇  Q J 9 7 6 2
♣  Q 10 8 4 2      S          ♣  9

              ♠  K Q J 10 8 5
              ♡  4 2
              ◇  10 4
              ♣  7 6 5
```

The best defence is to duck the spade lead from dummy, win the next spade with the ace and play a diamond, hoping to promote a trump trick for partner. The setting trick may then come from hearts.

The trouble with playing the ace on the first round is that it will collect only a low card from South, not an honour. This would make a trump promotion less likely. Of course, even if you duck the first spade, South can, in theory, thwart your plans by continuing with a low spade to knock out your ace. If South actually does this, try holding your cards closer to your chest.

There is no layout where it can be right to rush in with the ace of spades at once. Even in the unlikely event that South has eight spades headed by the K-J-10 and West Q-x, rising with the ace and playing a diamond can do no more than prevent the overtrick. South must always make six spade tricks to add to the four high card tricks in dummy.

35
Pairs, dealer North,
neither side vulnerable.

♠ A 8 6 2
♡ A 9 8 5 2
♢ A 4
♣ Q 2

WEST	NORTH	EAST	SOUTH
	1♡	No	2♣
No	2♡	No	2♠
No	4♠	No	4NT
No	5♠	No	6♠
No	No	Double	End

♠ Q J 7 4
♡ 3
♢ 5
♣ A K J 10 9 4 3

The play:
1 West leads ♡Q: **ace,** seven, three.

How should South plan the play?

36

♠ A 8 2
♡ J 3
♢ J 10 7 3
♣ K Q 4 3

Pairs, dealer South,
North-South vulnerable.

♠ Q 9 7 4 3
♡ 10 6 5 4
♢ 8 4
♣ J 2

WEST	NORTH	EAST	SOUTH
			1NT*
No	2NT	No	3NT
No	No	No	
*12-14			

The play:
1 West leads ♠4: two, **king,** ten
2 East returns ♠6: jack, **queen,** eight.

How should West continue?

37
Dealer East,
neither side vulnerable.

	♠	5 3 2
	♡	Q 6
	◇	7 3 2
	♣	10 7 6 5 3

WEST	NORTH	EAST	SOUTH
		1NT*	Double
No	2♣	No	4♠
No	No	No	

*12-14

	♠	K Q J 10 4
	♡	A K
	◇	A K J 4
	♣	K J

The play:

West leads the ten of hearts.

1 Calm down. Until the hand is over, forget about partner removing the biggest penalty double you have ever had against the weak no trump.
   You win with the ace of hearts
2 You lead ♠K: **East wins the ace**
3 East returns ♠7: **queen,** eight, three.

Plan the play.

38

	♠	J 8 4 2
	♡	J 8 5 4
	◇	K Q 7
	♣	6 2

Dealer South,
North-South vulnerable.

♠	9 6 3
♡	K 10 6
◇	6 4 3 2
♣	K Q J

WEST	NORTH	EAST	SOUTH
			1♣
No	1♡	No	3NT
No	No	No	

The play:

1 West leads ♣K: two, three, **ace**
2 South returns ♣10: **jack,** six, seven.

How should West continue?

35. En garde

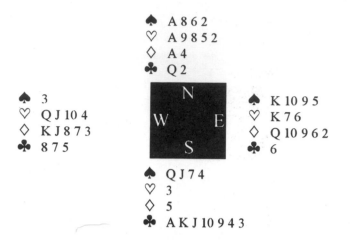

```
              ♠ A 8 6 2
              ♡ A 9 8 5 2
              ◇ A 4
              ♣ Q 2
  ♠ 3                      N              ♠ K 10 9 5
  ♡ Q J 10 4          W         E         ♡ K 7 6
  ◇ K J 8 7 3                             ◇ Q 10 9 6 2
  ♣ 8 7 5                 S              ♣ 6
              ♠ Q J 7 4
              ♡ 3
              ◇ 5
              ♣ A K J 10 9 4 3
```

In view of the double the trumps are sure to be stacked on your right, and you must hope they are no worse than 4-1. After taking the ace of hearts, lead a low spade to your queen, return to dummy with the ace of diamonds and lead another low spade to your jack. If East ducks twice, continue with a third spade to the ace and then run the clubs.

Should East rise with the king of spades on the second round and force you to ruff, play off the jack of spades, cross to dummy with the queen of clubs and draw the last trump before running the clubs.

The trap to avoid is playing the ace of spades early. To start with ace and another spade, or with a spade to the queen and a spade back to the ace, is to court disaster. East will play the king on the next trump lead and return a heart, forcing you to ruff with an honour, after which the hand will explode in your face.

Even without the double, you should tackle the trump suit in the same way. It would be greedy to try for an overtrick by running the jack or queen, playing for the remote chance of finding East with 10-9 doubleton.

36. Asleep at the wheel

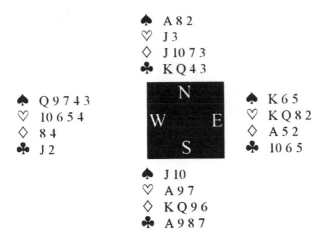

	♠ A 8 2	
	♡ J 3	
	◇ J 10 7 3	
	♣ K Q 4 3	
♠ Q 9 7 4 3		♠ K 6 5
♡ 10 6 5 4		♡ K Q 8 2
◇ 8 4		◇ A 5 2
♣ J 2		♣ 10 6 5
	♠ J 10	
	♡ A 9 7	
	◇ K Q 9 6	
	♣ A 9 8 7	

At the table a normally competent West fell asleep and continued with a third spade. Declarer now had nine tricks after knocking out the ◇ A.

With no entry to the spades. what can be gained by continuing with that suit? Rather than persevere with a futile line. West should switch. The obvious choice is to hearts as that is dummy's weakest holding. From West's point of view the heart switch may or may not break the contract. A spade continuation certainly will not.

It is true that East could have switched to the king of hearts at trick two. This would have been a wise move in practice and could also prove to be the only successful defence if West's spades were headed by the jack instead of the queen. However. on the actual layout the spade continuation should have worked out well when West was allowed to win the second trick. By switching to hearts at this point, West could have defeated the contract by two tricks for a top board.

Declarer might well have taken the ace of spades at trick 1. That would secure 3NT if spades were 4-4 while to duck could cost the game. South gambled that the defenders would not find the killing line. It pays to know your customers.

37. Partly by elimination

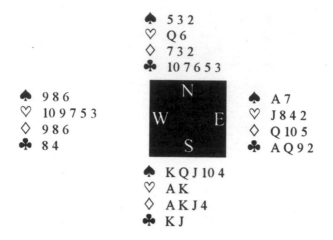

```
                   ♠  5 3 2
                   ♡  Q 6
                   ◊  7 3 2
                   ♣  10 7 6 5 3
  ♠  9 8 6                              ♠  A 7
  ♡  10 9 7 5 3          N              ♡  J 8 4 2
  ◊  9 8 6          W        E          ◊  Q 10 5
  ♣  8 4                 S              ♣  A Q 9 2
                   ♠  K Q J 10 4
                   ♡  A K
                   ◊  A K J 4
                   ♣  K J
```

Trap 1 : You must not draw the third round of trumps at this point. If diamonds are 4-2, you will need to ruff the fourth round of diamonds in dummy. To do this you may have to depend on a defensive error. For example, if East began with Q-x in diamonds and three spades, East must not ruff the jack of diamonds but wait to over-ruff dummy. This is to prevent your reaching dummy to lead a club towards your honours.

If diamonds are 3-3, it is still essential not to draw the outstanding trump immediately.

Trap 2 : You must not play the third round of diamonds until you have cashed the king of hearts. On the actual deal East is put on lead with the third diamond and must either open up the clubs or give you a ruff and discard by returning a heart. That is why dummy needs to retain a trump, to enable you to produce a partial elimination. This way you lose only one trump, one diamond and one club. If you fail to cash the king of hearts, East has an easy heart exit. Then you will have to lose two club tricks eventually by leading clubs from hand.

38. Your strength is their weakness

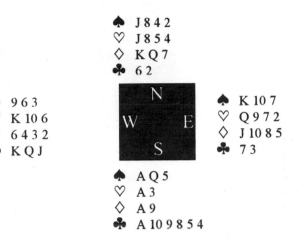

```
                    ♠ J 8 4 2
                    ♡ J 8 5 4
                    ◇ K Q 7
                    ♣ 6 2
    ♠ 9 6 3                          ♠ K 10 7
    ♡ K 10 6         N              ♡ Q 9 7 2
    ◇ 6 4 3 2      W   E            ◇ J 10 8 5
    ♣ K Q J          S              ♣ 7 3
                    ♠ A Q 5
                    ♡ A 3
                    ◇ A 9
                    ♣ A 10 9 8 5 4
```

Clearly West has to find a switch, and a heart looks the most promising
shot in view of dummy's weak holding. When dummy has bid a suit,
declarer often relies on that suit being adequately held for no-trump
purposes. Whenever dummy comes down with a weak holding in a suit
bid by dummy, be alert to switch to that suit if a switch is necessary.

Once West has decided to switch to hearts, there remains the question of
which card to lead. The defenders need three heart tricks, and West
should bear in mind the need to avoid blocking the suit. The correct
choice is the ten, which is the only card to defeat the contract on the
layout above. South wins with the ace and plays another club. West wins
and finishes South off with king and another heart.

Note that South can succeed if West starts with either the king or the six
of hearts. The lead of the ten leaves South without any answer.

39
Dealer North,
neither side vulnerable.

♠ K 7 6 3 2
♡ A J 10 7 6
♢ Q 10 4
♣ - - -

WEST	NORTH	EAST	SOUTH
	No	1♣	No
1♢	Dble	1NT*	2♠
3♣	4♠	Dble	End

*12-15 points

```
        N
  W           E
        S
```

♠ Q 9 8 4
♡ K 4 2
♢ 7 6
♣ K J 5 3

The play:
1 West leads ♣A: **you ruff in dummy,** East plays the two
2 ♠2 is led from dummy : ten, **queen,** five.

How should South continue?

40
Dealer South,
both sides vulnerable.

♠ J 8 7 5
♡ 7 4 3
♢ A K
♣ Q 8 6 2

WEST	NORTH	EAST	SOUTH
			1♠*
4♢	4♠	Double	End

*5+ suit

```
        N
  W           E
        S
```

♠ A Q 3
♡ A 8
♢ 7 4 3
♣ A J 10 5 3

The play:
1 West leads ♢2: **ace,** three, ten
2 ♠5 is played from dummy . . .

How should East defend?

41

Teams, dealer North,
both sides vulnerable.

♠ 8 6 4
♡ 9 6 3
♦ A K 6 3
♣ K 9 5

WEST	NORTH	EAST	SOUTH
	No	No	1♡
1♠	3♡*	No	4♡
No	No	No	

*N-S play 5-card majors and
North plays an aggressive game

♠ A K 10
♡ A J 10 8 4 2
♦ 5 2
♣ 7 3

The play:

1 West leads ♠3: four, nine, **ten**
2 **South plays ♡A**: *West discards ♣6.*

Plan South's play.

42

Teams, dealer North,
neither side vulnerable.

WEST	NORTH	EAST	SOUTH
	2♣ (1)	No	2NT (2)
No	3♦ (3)	No	3NT
No	No	No	

(1) 12-15 points, any 4-4-4-1 pattern
(2) Asking for the singleton
(3) Singleton diamond

What should West lead from :

♠ K Q J 6 4 3
♡ 10 9 2
♦ 3
♣ 7 3 2

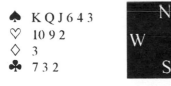

39. Majoring in card reading

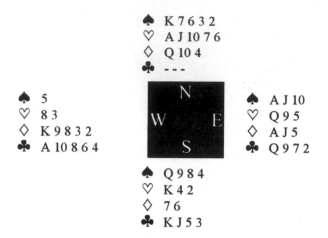

```
                    ♠ K 7 6 3 2
                    ♡ A J 10 7 6
                    ◊ Q 10 4
                    ♣ - - -
  ♠ 5                                    ♠ A J 10
  ♡ 8 3              N                   ♡ Q 9 5
  ◊ K 9 8 3 2     W     E                ◊ A J 5
  ♣ A 10 8 6 4       S                   ♣ Q 9 7 2
                    ♠ Q 9 8 4
                    ♡ K 4 2
                    ◊ 7 6
                    ♣ K J 5 3
```

South was lucky to escape an initial diamond lead and has already negotiated one hurdle successfully by playing a low spade from dummy at trick two (rather than the king of spades, hoping to pin an honour in the West hand).

When the queen of spades wins the second trick, South has to make a decision about how the trumps are breaking. Both the bidding and the play make it appear likely that the trumps will be 3-1 rather than 2-2. In that case South cannot afford to play a second trump before setting up the hearts for a diamond discard.

The key to the right play in hearts is again to be found in the bidding. East's 1NT and West's minor suit bidding make it highly likely that the heart length and the queen of hearts are with East. South should lead a low heart to the ace and run the jack of hearts on the way back. A third heart to the king is followed by a club ruff. The lead of an established heart winner from dummy allows South to discard a losing diamond as East ruffs with a natural trump winner.

40. Easy does it

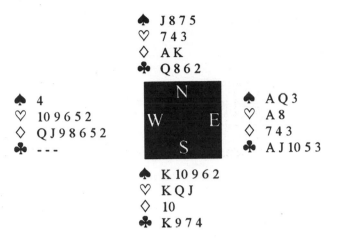

```
              ♠  J 8 7 5
              ♡  7 4 3
              ◇  A K
              ♣  Q 8 6 2

♠  4                              ♠  A Q 3
♡  10 9 6 5 2                     ♡  A 8
◇  Q J 9 8 6 5 2                  ◇  7 4 3
♣  - - -                          ♣  A J 10 5 3

              ♠  K 10 9 6 2
              ♡  K Q J
              ◇  10
              ♣  K 9 7 4
```

In practice East botched the defence by rising with the ace of spades to play ace and another club. East was hoping to give West a club ruff but West was out of trumps, and the declarer had no further trouble in making ten tricks.

After the hand, East rebuked West for seeking a club ruff (via the suit-preference lead of the *two* of diamonds) when holding only a singleton trump. But, of course, the two of diamonds lead could have been vital if East had held the diamond ace.

East was guilty of failing to make use of the available evidence. Since North-South were playing five-card majors, West could have no more than one trump. Rising with the ace of spades could have been costly if West's singleton were the jack. Further, if West could be placed with a void in clubs, it was obvious that South must have four clubs. All East had to do was cash the ace of hearts after coming in with the ace of spades, then sit back and wait for two club tricks.

It is one thing to work out what partner's lead means; it is another to apply the knowledge correctly. And it is never right to rebuke partner, even when you happen to be right.

41. Good news, bad news

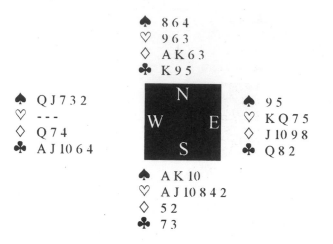

```
                    ♠  8 6 4
                    ♡  9 6 3
                    ◇  A K 6 3
                    ♣  K 9 5
♠  Q J 7 3 2          N              ♠  9 5
♡  - - -                              ♡  K Q 7 5
◇  Q 7 4         W        E          ◇  J 10 9 8
♣  A J 10 6 4        S               ♣  Q 8 2
                    ♠  A K 10
                    ♡  A J 10 8 4 2
                    ◇  5 2
                    ♣  7 3
```

The opening lead was a stroke of luck for the declarer, but it will do South no good to complain about North's overbidding and the unlucky trump split if North is able to retort, 'You shoulda made it!'

At the table the declarer failed when a trump was led to dummy's nine at trick three. East won the queen and returned a spade. On winning the next trump, East led a club to West's ace and ruffed the spade return for one down.

After the bad news at trick two, South knows that the contract cannot succeed unless the ace of clubs is with West. As West can be placed with five spades for the one spade overcall, South should foresee what will happen on a trump continuation.

The correct play is to lead a club at trick three. If West goes in with the ace, South can revert to playing trumps upon regaining the lead. If West ducks and the king of clubs wins, South must continue with a second club in order to cut the communications between East and West. The trumps can wait.

The name for this manoeuvre to sever the defence communications is 'The Scissors Coup'.

42. Out of sequence

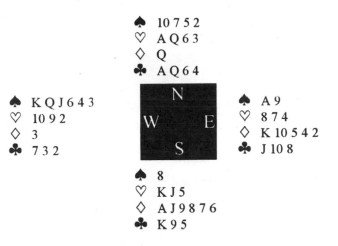

```
                  ♠  10 7 5 2
                  ♡  A Q 6 3
                  ◇  Q
                  ♣  A Q 6 4
                       N
♠ K Q J 6 4 3                        ♠  A 9
♡ 10 9 2          W         E        ♡  8 7 4
◇ 3                                  ◇  K 10 5 4 2
♣ 7 3 2                S             ♣  J 10 8
                  ♠  8
                  ♡  K J 5
                  ◇  A J 9 8 7 6
                  ♣  K 9 5
```

In an international match West led the ♡10 and declarer made 3NT
easily. A case can be made for a heart lead. A diamond is certainly out
(East would have doubled three diamonds with very strong diamonds),
and a major suit lead is better than a lead from those anaemic clubs.

Take half marks for a heart lead, and half marks for leading a spade
honour (which could work if South were void but blocks the suit here).
To earn full marks you have to lead a *low* spade. When you are leading a
suit bid by declarer or dummy, by all means lead top from a four-card
sequence. With only a three-card sequence in a suit where an opponent
has at least four cards, lead fourth-highest rather than top of sequence
against no trumps.

The lead of the low card may yield a different benefit. In the 1971
Bermuda Bowl, Board 2 of Round 10 had this club distribution :

```
               ♣  A 10 8 5
    ♣  K Q J 7 2          ♣  9 6
               ♣  4 3
```

Against 3NT, Tim Seres of Australia found the devastating *two* of clubs
lead through dummy's first bid suit. Declarer naturally finessed the eight
and the nine won. Clubs were continued and as West had a side entry,
the defenders made five tricks. No other defence would have prevailed.

43
Dealer South,
North-South vulnerable.

♠ A Q
♡ 9 6 2
◇ J 6 4
♣ K Q J 10 5

WEST	NORTH	EAST	SOUTH
			1NT
No	3NT	All pass	

♠ K 4 3
♡ A K 5
◇ A 7 3
♣ 6 4 3 2

The play:
West leads ◇5.
Plan South's play.
(If you play low in dummy, East produces the ten; if you play dummy's jack, it is covered by East.)

44
Pairs, dealer South,
East-West vulnerable.

♠ J 10 5 3
♡ 8 6 5 2
◇ 5
♣ A 10 4 3

WEST	NORTH	EAST	SOUTH
			1NT*
No	No	No	
*12-14			

♠ Q 9 7 4
♡ K Q 9
◇ K J 8 7
♣ K 6

The play:
1 West leads ♣5: three, **king,** eight
2 East leads ◇7: **queen,** ten, five
3 **South leads ♠A:** eight, three, seven
4 **South leads ♠K:** *West discards ♣2*
5 South leads ♠6: *West discards ◇3,* ♠J from dummy . . .

How should East defend?

45
Teams, dealer North,
neither side vulnerable.

♠ 9 3
♡ A 2
♢ J 9 3
♣ A K 10 7 6 3

WEST	NORTH	EAST	SOUTH
	1♣	Dble	2♠ (1)
3♡	4♣	4♡	4♠
No	No	Dble	End

(1) Fit-showing jump

♠ Q J 10 6 4 2
♡ 8 7
♢ A
♣ Q 9 4 2

West leads ♡Q. Plan South's play.

46
Dealer South,
both sides vulnerable.

♠ 10 7
♡ A 10 7 5
♢ A 9 5
♣ Q 10 6 2

WEST	NORTH	EAST	SOUTH
			1NT*
No	2♣	No	2♢
No	2NT	No	3NT

*12-14

♠ K Q 5
♡ 8 4
♢ J 10 6 3 2
♣ A 8 4

The play:
1 West leads ♣4: seven, **queen,** three
2 **East plays** ♣K: six from South, two from West.

Plan East's defence.

43. On the block where you live

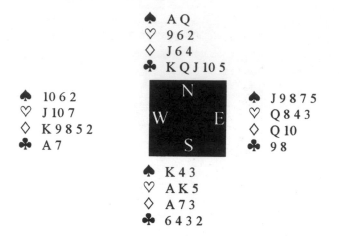

```
              ♠ A Q
              ♡ 9 6 2
              ◊ J 6 4
              ♣ K Q J 10 5
  ♠ 10 6 2                        ♠ J 9 8 7 5
  ♡ J 10 7                        ♡ Q 8 4 3
  ◊ K 9 8 5 2                     ◊ Q 10
  ♣ A 7                           ♣ 9 8
              ♠ K 4 3
              ♡ A K 5
              ◊ A 7 3
              ♣ 6 4 3 2
```

It is tempting to play the jack of diamonds from dummy at trick one and
that is what the declarer did in practice. East covered with the queen
and South ducked. When East continued with the ten of diamonds,
South again played low, but West overtook with the king and cleared the
diamond suit. West regained the lead with the ace of clubs and cashed
the diamonds for one down.

Declarer does not need two diamond tricks for the contract and so the
aim is to guard against the diamond attack. There is no problem if the
diamonds are 4-3, of course. If they are 5-2, playing the jack works
when West has led from K-Q-x-x-x, while playing low from dummy and
winning with the ace works when West has led from K-x-x-x-x or from
Q-x-x-x-x. Then East has Q-x or K-x and playing the ace at trick one
blocks the suit. As the latter situation is twice as likely, it is correct to
play low from dummy and take the ace of diamonds at trick one.

44. Making matchpoints from mangling

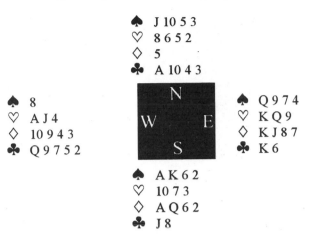

```
                    ♠ J 10 5 3
                    ♡ 8 6 5 2
                    ◇ 5
                    ♣ A 10 4 3
        ♠ 8                          ♠ Q 9 7 4
        ♡ A J 4                      ♡ K Q 9
        ◇ 10 9 4 3                   ◇ K J 8 7
        ♣ Q 9 7 5 2                  ♣ K 6
                    ♠ A K 6 2
                    ♡ 10 7 3
                    ◇ A Q 6 2
                    ♣ J 8
```

South has already shown up with thirteen points (A-K in spades, A-Q in diamonds) and cannot have more than a jack extra. West's two of clubs indicates the lead was from five clubs, which in turn means that declarer has no chance of making 1NT unless holding the jack of clubs.

If East wins with the queen of spades and returns a diamond, South wins, runs the jack of clubs, and crosses to the ten of spades to cash the ace of clubs. East can prevent this either by ducking the jack of spades or by winning and returning the fourth spade to eliminate the entry to dummy. When East later regains the lead it would be wise to return the six of clubs, thus making it easy for West to duck declarer's jack.

The declarer mangled the hand, of course. Unblocking the jack of clubs at trick one would have allowed South to score two club tricks by finessing the ten later. Alternatively, after the top spades were cashed, the jack of clubs could have been led before the third round of spades. It would not be considered polite to mention these points or to extol the virtues of Stayman. Suffice to note South's name in your little black book under the heading 'Players not to be sought as partners'.

45. Severance pays

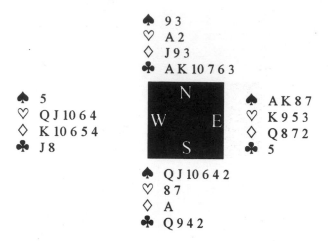

```
              ♠ 9 3
              ♡ A 2
              ◊ J 9 3
              ♣ A K 10 7 6 3
♠ 5                              ♠ A K 8 7
♡ Q J 10 6 4      N              ♡ K 9 5 3
◊ K 10 6 5 4   W     E           ◊ Q 8 7 2
♣ J 8             S              ♣ 5
              ♠ Q J 10 6 4 2
              ♡ 8 7
              ◊ A
              ♣ Q 9 4 2
```

The average player takes the ace of hearts and immediately tackles trumps. The expert play, however, is to duck the first heart. On the actual lie of the cards this is a very necessary safeguard.

At one table in a teams match the declarer won the ace of hearts and played a spade. East won with the king and switched to the singleton club. On regaining the lead with the ace of spades, East led a low heart to West. The club return was ruffed to put four spades one down.

At the other table the declarer ducked the heart lead, thereby thwarting this defence. There was no longer any entry to the West hand.

It could cost to duck the first heart if West had two low trumps plus a singleton club and switched to the club at trick two. However, West might have led the singleton club initially and in view of East's two doubles, East is the one far more likely to hold a singleton club along with four trumps.

46. What's the hurry?

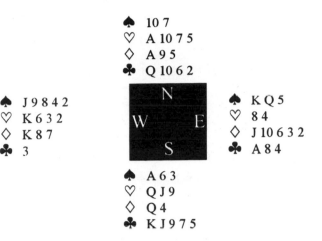

```
                    ♠  10 7
                    ♡  A 10 7 5
                    ◊  A 9 5
                    ♣  Q 10 6 2

♠  J 9 8 4 2            N            ♠  K Q 5
♡  K 6 3 2                           ♡  8 4
◊  K 8 7          W          E       ◊  J 10 6 3 2
♣  3                    S            ♣  A 8 4

                    ♠  A 6 3
                    ♡  Q J 9
                    ◊  Q 4
                    ♣  K J 9 7 5
```

East's problem is whether to continue spades, playing West to have led from A-9-8-4-2, or whether to switch to diamonds.

After a little thought, East should realise that a switch to the three of diamonds is best. If West did begin with five spades headed by the ace, declarer can make no more than eight tricks in the red suits before letting East in with the ace of clubs. Therefore East has time for two bites at the cherry.

At the table, East hastily played a third spade. Declarer won, knocked out the ace of clubs and took the heart finesse for ten tricks.

The presence of the nine of diamonds in dummy precludes a lead of the diamond jack at trick three. On the lead of a low diamond declarer should, in practice, rise with the queen. If not, declarer is either a beginner or has seen your cards. In the former case, you have a sufficient edge; in the latter you know what to do.

Three down should induce in North-South a healthy respect for your defence. They will be less eager to bid game against you on such flimsy values in future.

47
Dealer North,
neither side vulnerable.

♠ J 7 5
♡ J 10
♢ A K 3 2
♣ A J 5 2

WEST	NORTH	EAST	SOUTH
	1NT	2♠	4♡
No	No	No	

♠ 9 6
♡ A Q 9 8 7 3
♢ 8
♣ K 10 9 3

The play:
1 **West leads ♠Q:** five, eight, six
2 West plays ♠4: seven, **ten,** nine
3 East plays ♠A: South ruffs with ♡9, **West over-ruffs with ♡K**
4 West leads ♡4: **jack,** five, three

How should South continue?

48
Pairs, dealer South,
East-West vulnerable.

♠ K 6 4 2
♡ 8 2
♢ Q 4 3
♣ J 9 6 2

WEST	NORTH	EAST	SOUTH
			1♢
No	1♠	No	2NT*
No	No	No	

*17-18 points

♠ A Q 10 9 5
♡ 10 3
♢ A 7 2
♣ 8 4 3

The play:
1 West leads ♡5: two, ten, **king**
2 South leads ♢6 to dummy's queen, West playing the eight . . .

Plan East's defence.
(If East ducks, diamonds are continued)

49
Teams, dealer South,
neither side vulnerable.

♠ Q 9 7 6
♡ J 8 7 5
♢ J 10
♣ Q 6 5

WEST	NORTH	EAST	SOUTH
			2NT
No	3♣*	No	3♢
No	3NT	All pass	

*Stayman

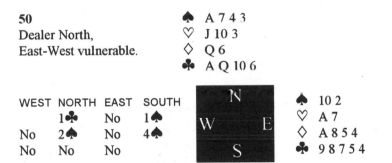

♠ A K 4
♡ A 9
♢ K 9 3
♣ A K 9 4 3

The play:
1 West leads ♢6: **jack,** five, nine.

How should South continue?

50
Dealer North,
East-West vulnerable.

♠ A 7 4 3
♡ J 10 3
♢ Q 6
♣ A Q 10 6

WEST	NORTH	EAST	SOUTH
	1♣	No	1♠
No	2♠	No	4♠
No	No	No	

♠ 10 2
♡ A 7
♢ A 8 5 4
♣ 9 8 7 5 4

West leads the king of hearts. Plan East's defence.

47. Reducing a two-way guess to no-guess

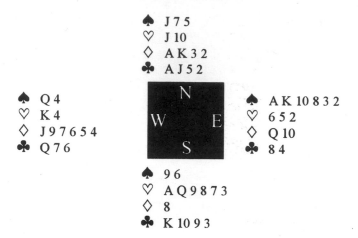

```
              ♠ J 7 5
              ♡ J 10
              ◇ A K 3 2
              ♣ A J 5 2

♠ Q 4              N              ♠ A K 10 8 3 2
♡ K 4                             ♡ 6 5 2
◇ J 9 7 6 5 4  W       E          ◇ Q 10
♣ Q 7 6              S            ♣ 8 4

              ♠ 9 6
              ♡ A Q 9 8 7 3
              ◇ 8
              ♣ K 10 9 3
```

You have lost three tricks and need to avoid a club loser. You might be inclined to place the ♣Q with East for that 2♠ overcall. On the other hand, as East is long in spades, East is likely to be shorter in clubs. If West has more clubs than East, then the ♣Q is more likely to be with the length.

Fortunately you can improve your chances considerably beyond a guess as to which opponent is more likely to hold the ♣Q. After winning with the ♡J, cash the ♡10 and then play ◇A, ◇K and ruff a diamond. When you draw the last trump, you know all you need to know.

East began with six spades, three hearts and two diamonds. East must therefore hold exactly two clubs. East could still hold the ♣Q, of course, but no guesswork is needed. Just cash your remaining trumps and watch for the missing three diamonds. West can discard two diamonds safely but then it is all over. With four cards remaining, the position will be:

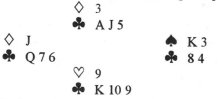

```
              ◇ 3
              ♣ A J 5
◇ J              ♠ K 3
♣ Q 7 6          ♣ 8 4
              ♡ 9
              ♣ K 10 9
```

When you lead your last trump, if West lets a club go, discard dummy's diamond and ♣K and ♣A sees you home, no matter where the ♣Q lies.

48. Wait for the signal

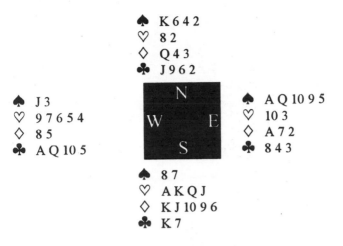

```
                ♠ K 6 4 2
                ♡ 8 2
                ◇ Q 4 3
                ♣ J 9 6 2

♠ J 3              N            ♠ A Q 10 9 5
♡ 9 7 6 5 4    W     E         ♡ 10 3
◇ 8 5                          ◇ A 7 2
♣ A Q 10 5        S            ♣ 8 4 3

                ♠ 8 7
                ♡ A K Q J
                ◇ K J 10 9 6
                ♣ K 7
```

East should hold up the ace of diamonds until the third round. There can be no urgency to return a heart. If West has the top hearts South cannot come to eight tricks without the diamond suit. At most South could have four clubs, two diamonds and a heart. In any event it is unlikely that the defence can run the hearts. West would not lead the 5 from A-Q-J-x-x or Q-J-9-x-x (the normal lead would be the queen).

Holding up the ace of diamonds allows East the benefit of a signal from West how the defence should continue. On the third diamond, West will discard the ten of clubs or the four of hearts, either of which gives the right message. East can then switch to the eight of clubs, leading a high spot card to deny interest in the suit led. West will win and return the jack of spades. The defence will now come to three spades (five if declarer goes up with dummy's king), two clubs and a diamond.

South's 2NT rebid is somewhat off-beat, but the no-trump syndrome in the pairs game is as incurable as the common cold. Note that if East takes the ace of diamonds and returns a heart, declarer wraps up eight tricks instantly.

49. Safe and sound

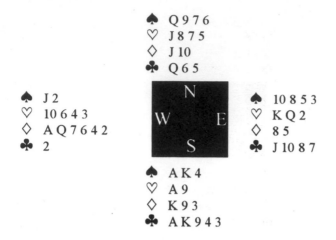

```
              ♠ Q 9 7 6
              ♡ J 8 7 5
              ◇ J 10
              ♣ Q 6 5

  ♠ J 2              N           ♠ 10 8 5 3
  ♡ 10 6 4 3    W       E        ♡ K Q 2
  ◇ A Q 7 6 4 2                  ◇ 8 5
  ♣ 2               S            ♣ J 10 8 7

              ♠ A K 4
              ♡ A 9
              ◇ K 9 3
              ♣ A K 9 4 3
```

The straightforward method of playing the hand is to cash the queen of clubs and continue with a club to the ace or king. If the suit breaks 3-2 there is no problem. If West proves to have four clubs, you can safely concede a club trick and establish the suit. If East has four clubs, you can always fall back on the spades. This method of play will succeed nine times out of ten.

Once East follows to the first club, however, you can make certain of nine tricks by inserting your nine of clubs if East plays low on the second round. If East plays an honour and West shows out, return to dummy with the third round of spades and take the marked club finesse.

On the actual deal it would work equally well to finesse the nine of clubs on the first round but playing the queen first has the advantage of picking up all the tricks when West has the jack or ten of clubs singleton and when East has 10-x or J-x in clubs.

50. Observe the Golden Rule

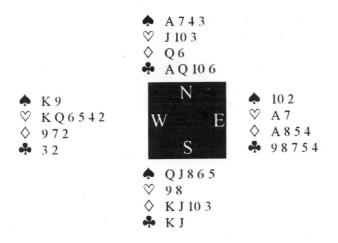

♠ A 7 4 3
♥ J 10 3
♦ Q 6
♣ A Q 10 6

♠ K 9
♥ K Q 6 5 4 2
♦ 9 7 2
♣ 3 2

♠ 10 2
♥ A 7
♦ A 8 5 4
♣ 9 8 7 5 4

♠ Q J 8 6 5
♥ 9 8
♦ K J 10 3
♣ K J

The defence will vary according to the standard of the player.

The novice will play the seven of hearts and block the suit. The contract will still be defeated if West holds the king of diamonds, but on the actual deal, declarer will succeed.

The average player, recognizing that the lead is from K-Q, overtakes the king with the ace and returns the seven of hearts. This works on the deal above for West wins and plays a third heart. East ruffs with the 10, an uppercut which knocks out one of declarer's trump honours and so produces a trump trick for West. But suppose South began with, say
♠ K Q J 9 8 6   ♥ 9 8   ♦ J 10 9   ♣ K J.
It will not be easy for West, after winning the second heart, to find the diamond switch away from the king. On any continuation but a diamond at trick 3, declarer has ten tricks.

The expert covers every contingency After overtaking the king of hearts cash the ace of diamonds and then revert to hearts. No matter what the position, West should be able to find the correct continuation. Expert defence aims to clarify the position for partner whenever possible.

Golden Rule of Defence: **Don't give partner a chance to go wrong.** (If you do, partner will grab that chance!)

51
Teams, dealer North,
East-West vulnerable.

	♠	A 9 7 2
	♡	Q 9 7 6
	◇	A
	♣	A Q 5 2

WEST	NORTH	EAST	SOUTH
	1♣	No	1◇
No	1♡	No	1♠*
No	3♠	No	6NT**
No	No	No	

*Fourth suit forcing
**4NT for aces would
be prudent here

	♠	K Q 5
	♡	A K 3
	◇	K Q 7 5 2
	♣	9 4

The play:
1 West leads ◇J: **ace,** six, two
2 ♠2 from dummy: three, **king,** six
3 **South leads ◇K:** three, *dummy discards ♣2, East discards ♣6.*

How should South continue?

52

	♠	7 4
	♡	K 7 3
	◇	6 5
	♣	A J 9 4 3 2

Dealer West,
both sides vulnerable.

♠ K 10 9 3	
♡ 8 4	
◇ K Q J 3 2	
♣ K 7	

WEST	NORTH	EAST	SOUTH
1◇	No	No	Dble
No	3♣	No	3NT
No	No	No	

The play:
1 **West leads ◇K:** five, four, eight
2 **West plays ◇Q:** six, ten, nine.

How should West continue?

53
Teams, dealer West,
both sides vulnerable.

♠ A K Q 2
♡ 7 5
♢ A 9 8
♣ 9 8 6 5

WEST	NORTH	EAST	SOUTH
1♠	No	1NT	No
2♡	No	No	3♢
No	No	No	

♠ J 4
♡ 9 6 2
♢ K J 6 5 3 2
♣ K 3

The play:
1 West leads ♡J: five, **ace**, two
2 East switches to ♣4: king, **ace**, five
3 **West plays ♡K:** seven, three, six
4 West plays ♣J: six, **queen**, three
5 East returns ♣7 . . .

How do you plan the play from here? How will you handle the trumps?

54
Teams, dealer South,
North-South vulnerable.

♠ 7
♡ K 8 7 6 4
♢ K 6
♣ Q J 8 7 2

WEST	NORTH	EAST	SOUTH		♠ J 6 4
			1♠		♡ A J 5
No	2♡	No	2NT*		♢ 9 8 7 4 2
No	3♣	No	3NT		♣ 9 3
No	No	No	*15-17		

The play:
1 West leads ♢3: six, seven, **queen**
2 South leads ♣5: six, **queen**, nine
3 ♣2 is led from dummy: three, king, **ace**
4 West leads ♡Q: king, **ace**, three
5 **East leads ♡J:** nine, two, four.

How should East continue?

85

51. Success without finesse

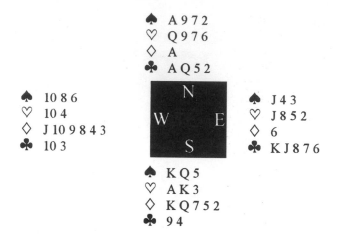

```
              ♠  A 9 7 2
              ♡  Q 9 7 6
              ◇  A
              ♣  A Q 5 2

  ♠  10 8 6         N          ♠  J 4 3
  ♡  10 4                      ♡  J 8 5 2
  ◇  J 10 9 8 4 3  W    E      ◇  6
  ♣  10 3                      ♣  K J 8 7 6
                    S
              ♠  K Q 5
              ♡  A K 3
              ◇  K Q 7 5 2
              ♣  9 4
```

You have ten tricks in top cards and the diamond split means there are no more tricks from that suit. If both majors are 3-3, you have twelve tricks. If one major is 3-3 and the club finesse works, that will do, too. Being short in diamonds, East figures to have length in clubs and if so, the ♣K is more likely to be with East than West.

If East has four or more cards in each major, no squeeze will operate as East sits over dummy. There is no sure play but your best hope if the majors are not both 3-3 is to find East with 3-4 or 4-3 in the majors. If that situation exists, you do not need the club finesse.

Cash your third diamond, discarding another club from dummy. Then test the majors. Suppose you try spades first and find they are 3-3. Cash the last spade and then test the hearts, ending in dummy. When East turns up with four hearts, play your last heart and score the last two tricks in clubs. If you try hearts first and find East with four hearts, then cash the spades, play the thirteenth and endplay East with the fourth heart.

This line also works if East began with the ♣K and 5+ cards in one major as long as the other major is 3-3. On your diamond winners and the extra trick from the 3-3 major, East will have to discard from the long major or bare the ♣K.

52. Diamonds are not forever

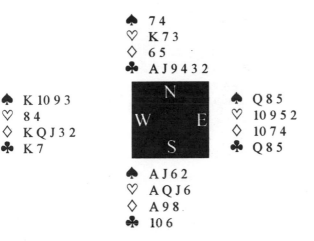

```
                    ♠  7 4
                    ♡  K 7 3
                    ◇  6 5
                    ♣  A J 9 4 3 2
    ♠  K 10 9 3                        ♠  Q 8 5
    ♡  8 4                             ♡  10 9 5 2
    ◇  K Q J 3 2                       ◇  10 7 4
    ♣  K 7                             ♣  Q 8 5
                    ♠  A J 6 2
                    ♡  A Q J 6
                    ◇  A 9 8
                    ♣  10 6
```

The diamond position should be clear, East having started with 10-7-4 and South with A-9-8. If East had 10-4 doubleton, South with A-9-8-7 would have won the second round of diamonds to create an extra trick there. If you play a third diamond, you will dislodge the ace and set up two winners but where is your re-entry to cash those winners? Your ♠K may be an entry but unless partner has the ♠A (not too likely on the bidding), declarer is likely to have wrapped up at least nine tricks before you can enjoy the ♠K.

Your best chance is to find partner with an entry in clubs and the ♠Q. If that situation exists, a spade switch will work. You lead the ♠10 or ♠3 to East's queen and declarer's ace. When East comes on lead with the ♣Q, a spade return will give you two or three more tricks, three if declarer began with A-J-x. If it turns out that declarer's spades are headed by the A-Q, it is highly improbable that you had any hope of defeating 3NT.

There is a strong clue that East does have a high spade. On the second diamond, why did East follow with the ten rather than the seven? This unnecessarily high card should be taken as a suit-preference signal: high card for the high suit. With nothing in spades, East should play the diamonds in normal order from the bottom up.

53. Lots of pointers from the points

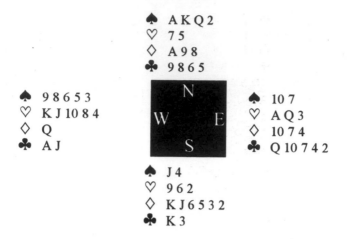

```
              ♠  A K Q 2
              ♡  7 5
              ♢  A 9 8
              ♣  9 8 6 5

♠  9 8 6 5 3         N          ♠  10 7
♡  K J 10 8 4                   ♡  A Q 3
♢  Q           W         E      ♢  10 7 4
♣  A J                          ♣  Q 10 7 4 2
                     S
              ♠  J 4
              ♡  9 6 2
              ♢  K J 6 5 3 2
              ♣  K 3
```

Your side has 21 HCP and they began with 19 HCP. You have seen most of their high cards from the early play. You know that West began with K-J in hearts and A-J in clubs while East has shown up with the ♡A, ♣Q and the ♡Q by inference (West would have led the ♡K from K-Q-J). The only high card missing is the ♢Q, almost certainly with West to justify the opening bid. In addition, the ♢Q would give East 10 HCP, and East might then have done more than just 1NT.

West's bidding indicates at least five spades and four hearts. Two clubs have been seen. West's original pattern is almost certain to be one of the following: 5-4-2-2, 5-4-1-3, 5-5-1-2 or 6-4-1-2. If it is a 5-4-2-2 with Q-x in diamonds, you are bound to fail no matter how you play. Ruff low and West over-ruffs; ruff with the ♢K and the defence will score a trump trick somehow.

In the other cases, West holds a singleton diamond, likely to be the ♢Q on the previous analysis. It is therefore essential to ruff the third club with the king of diamonds if West started with only two clubs. When West shows out, continue with a low trump. Capture the queen with the ace and then finesse against East's remaining ♢10-x. If West follows to the third club, your play still works if West has the ♢Q bare.

54. Haste makes waste

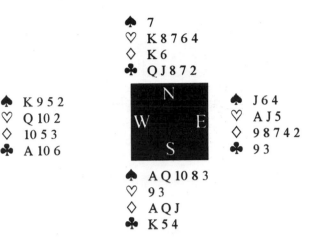

```
              ♠ 7
              ♡ K 8 7 6 4
              ◇ K 6
              ♣ Q J 8 7 2
♠ K 9 5 2                        ♠ J 6 4
♡ Q 10 2          N              ♡ A J 5
◇ 10 5 3      W       E          ◇ 9 8 7 4 2
♣ A 10 6          S              ♣ 9 3
              ♠ A Q 10 8 3
              ♡ 9 3
              ◇ A Q J
              ♣ K 5 4
```

At the table East woodenly returned a diamond, giving the declarer an easy passage. Dummy's king won, a third heart was played, and the defenders made only three hearts and a club.

Had East returned a spade at trick six, that would have established a fifth trick for the defence.

After the hand East complained about West leading such a poor suit. That was unreasonable. The bidding made a diamond lead almost mandatory for West.

East also claimed to be unable to tell whether West held the ace of diamonds or the king of spades, but this excuse does not hold water. With the ace of diamonds, West could always cash it when in with the third round of hearts. With the king of spades, West needed a spade lead from East.

Even if South has a strong spade hand such as

$$♠ A K Q 9 8 \quad ♡ 9 3 \quad ◇ Q J 10 \quad ♣ K 5 4$$

the contract will be defeated on a spade return. The heart ten is marked with West, of course, because of South's failure to support hearts.

PART 3: Advanced Level

55
Dealer East,
East-West vulnerable.

   ♠ 10 6 5
   ♡ Q 7
   ◇ K Q 7 4
   ♣ A J 3 2

North opens a weak no trump
and the partnership reaches:
(a) Four spades
(b) Five spades.

```
        N
  W           E
        S
```

   ♠ A 8 7 4 3
   ♡ K 8
   ◇ A J 6
   ♣ K Q 9

In each case West leads the ♡3 to the ace and East returns a heart.
Plan the play for both contracts.

56

   ♠ A J 10 9 7
   ♡ 7 6 5 4 3
   ◇ A 10
   ♣ J

Teams, dealer South,
East-West vulnerable.

♠ Q 4 3 2
♡ K J 10 9
◇ K 7 6 2
♣ 4

```
        N
  W           E
        S
```

WEST	NORTH	EAST	SOUTH
			3NT*
No	No	No	

*Solid minor suit with perhaps a
little outside strength

The play:
1 West leads ♡J : **East wins the ace,** South drops the queen
2 East returns ♡8 : *South discards ◇8*
3 **West cashes ♡10:** *South discards ◇9*
4 **West cashes ♡K:** *East discards ♠5, South discards ◇5.*

How should West continue?

57
Teams, dealer North,
both sides vulnerable.

♠ Q 6 5 4
♥ A K Q 7
♦ 9 8 5
♣ 6 2

WEST	NORTH	EAST	SOUTH
	No	No	1♥
No	3♥	No	5♥
No	6♥	All pass	

♠ - - -
♥ 10 9 6 4 3
♦ A K J 4
♣ A K J 9

The play:
1 West leads ♥2: **ace**, eight, three
2 **♥K is played from dummy:** jack, four, five.

How should declarer play?
What would your answer be at match-pointed pairs —
a) in a weak field?   b) in a strong field?

58

♠ K 2
♥ 10 7
♦ A K 6 5 2
♣ 7 6 5 4

Teams, dealer East,
East-West vulnerable.

♠ A Q 7 6
♥ J 8 6 3
♦ 10 4
♣ K 10 2

WEST	NORTH	EAST	SOUTH
		No	1NT*
No	2NT	No	3NT
No	No	No	

*12-14

The play:
1 West leads ♠6: two, nine, **jack**
2 **South plays ♦Q:** ten, two, three
3 South leads ♦7: four, **ace**, jack
4 **Dummy plays ♦K:** eight, nine. *West discards ♥8 (discouraging)*
5 **Dummy plays ♦6:** *East discards ♠10 (= values in hearts), ♥2, ♥3*
6 **Dummy plays ♦5:** *East discards ♠4, South ♣8 . . .*

What should West discard?

55. It costs nothing to try

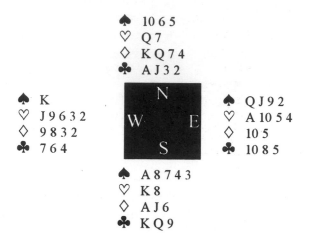

```
              ♠ 10 6 5
              ♡ Q 7
              ◇ K Q 7 4
              ♣ A J 3 2

♠ K                           ♠ Q J 9 2
♡ J 9 6 3 2                   ♡ A 10 5 4
◇ 9 8 3 2                     ◇ 10 5
♣ 7 6 4                       ♣ 10 8 5

              ♠ A 8 7 4 3
              ♡ K 8
              ◇ A J 6
              ♣ K Q 9
```

a) In four spades your only concern is to avoid losing three trump tricks.
There will be no problem if trumps are 3-2, but that does not mean you
should simply bang out ace and another trump and hope for the best.
You can give yourself a slight extra chance by crossing to dummy and
leading the ten of trumps. That cannot cost in any spade layout and is
the genuine way to hold your trump losers to two if East started with
K-Q-J-2 and West with the singleton nine. But leading the ten also gives
you a psychological chance, for East may err and cover from K-Q-9-2,
K-J-9-2 or Q-J-9-2.

At the table East did cover the ten, thereby telescoping three trump
tricks into two. There was nothing to gain by covering, but the habits of
a lifetime are not easily broken. A sound principle is not to cover where
partner is marked with a doubleton, singleton or void in the suit led
unless you are definitely creating an extra trick for yourself.

b) In five spades there is no genuine chance for the contract, but the best
shot is to lead a low trump towards the ten. You hope that West will
play high from J-9-2 or Q-9-2, thus colliding with partner's doubleton
honours and limiting your trump losers to one. This is not much of a
hope and it will not work against competent opposition, but who plays
against such opposition all the time?

56. One small hope

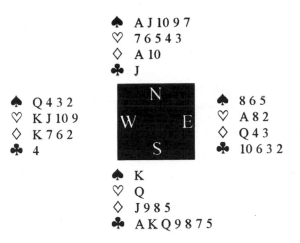

```
              ♠ A J 10 9 7
              ♡ 7 6 5 4 3
              ◇ A 10
              ♣ J

  ♠ Q 4 3 2        N          ♠ 8 6 5
  ♡ K J 10 9                  ♡ A 8 2
  ◇ K 7 6 2    W       E      ◇ Q 4 3
  ♣ 4              S          ♣ 10 6 3 2

              ♠ K
              ♡ Q
              ◇ J 9 8 5
              ♣ A K Q 9 8 7 5
```

South is marked with a long and solid club suit, but some solid suits are more solid than others. Clearly there is no hope for the defence if South's clubs are as good as A-K-Q-10-x-x-x. West must defend on the assumption that East has four clubs headed by the ten.

Even then declarer may be able to make 3NT if there is an entry to the South hand after cashing the jack of clubs in dummy. Holding the king of diamonds, West can see that the only possible entry declarer can hold outside clubs is the king of spades. Indeed South is likely to hold the king in view of East's discard of the five of spades at trick three.

West should therefore switch to a spade, hoping that South has the king singleton, in an attempt to knock out South's entry before the clubs can be unblocked. This is the only defence that offers any hope of defeating the contract.

57. Safest needle in the haystack

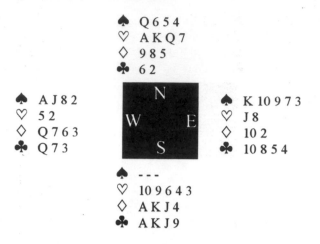

♠ Q 6 5 4
♥ A K Q 7
♦ 9 8 5
♣ 6 2

♠ A J 8 2
♥ 5 2
♦ Q 7 6 3
♣ Q 7 3

♠ K 10 9 7 3
♥ J 8
♦ 10 2
♣ 10 8 5 4

♠ - - -
♥ 10 9 6 4 3
♦ A K J 4
♣ A K J 9

At the table declarer finessed the ♣J at trick three. West won and tried to cash the ♠A. South ruffed and played ♣A and ♣K, pitching a diamond from dummy. Next came the ♦A and ♦K followed by a diamond ruff. As neither the ♦Q nor the ♣10 had appeared, declarer had to go down.

The declarer was unlucky, to be sure, but there was one extra chance available : the ten of diamonds coming down doubleton. There are many possible lines of play and the following offers the best chance of success. First, play off the ace and king of diamonds. If either the queen or the ten of diamonds drops, you are home. If a diamond honour has not appeared, continue with the ace and king of clubs and ruff the nine of clubs in dummy. Then lead a diamond from the table towards your J-4. This line is bound to succeed unless West has four or more diamonds headed by the queen and ten. Even then success will be yours if the queen of clubs drops in three rounds.

(a) At pairs in a weak field, not many will reach the slam and you should still adopt the safest line.
(b) In a strong field most pairs will bid 6♥ and you should try for an overtrick. The best bet is the diamond finesse. If it fails, cash a top diamond to see if the ten appears. If not, cash another top diamond and, if the suit does not break 3-3, ruff the fourth diamond and take the club finesse.

94

58. Keeping in contact with partner

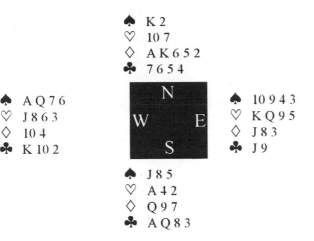

```
              ♠  K 2
              ♡  10 7
              ◊  A K 6 5 2
              ♣  7 6 5 4
♠  A Q 7 6                        ♠  10 9 4 3
♡  J 8 6 3                        ♡  K Q 9 5
◊  10 4                           ◊  J 8 3
♣  K 10 2                         ♣  J 9
              ♠  J 8 5
              ♡  A 4 2
              ◊  Q 9 7
              ♣  A Q 8 3
```

Partner has indicated values in hearts by the suit-preference discard of the ♠10 (a useful signalling system). You can deduce that East began with four spades. East has discarded two spades but would keep one to return to you. With five spades originally, East would have held on to all of them.

Of South's strength (13-14 for accepting the 2NT invitation), only the ♠J and ◊Q have been seen so far and so South has another 10-11 HCP. If you place East with ♡K-Q or ♡A-Q, South must have A-Q of clubs.

Given East's liking for hearts, South's suit is probably clubs. If South began with four or five clubs, you cannot afford to discard a club. If you do, South can lose the club finesse to you but will score an extra club trick after you cash your three spades.

You cannot afford another heart discard either as this lays you open to an endplay in clubs. At the table West did discard a third heart. Declarer then cashed the ace of hearts and exited with a spade to score two club tricks for the contract at the end.

As long as you discard the ♠7 on the fifth diamond, the defence can prevail regardless of declarer's continuation. If declarer plays a spade, you can cash your other spade winner, East discarding a heart, and exit safely with the ♡J.

59

Teams, dealer East,
North-South vulnerable.

♠ 10 8 7 4
♡ A 8 6 3 2
♢ J 2
♣ A 5

WEST	NORTH	EAST	SOUTH
		No	2NT
No	3♣ (1)	No	3♠
No	4NT (2)	No	5♣ (3)
No	6♠	All pass	

(1) Stayman
(2) Roman Key Card Blackwood
(3) 0 or 3 key cards

♠ A K Q 5
♡ K 5
♢ A 10 8 4
♣ K J 10

West leads the jack of hearts. How should South plan the play?

60

Teams, dealer North,
East-West vulnerable.

♠ 6
♡ A K 9 5
♢ Q J 3
♣ A K Q 8 2

♠ K Q 9 5 3
♡ 8 6 4 3 2
♢ K 8 5
♣ - - -

WEST	NORTH	EAST	SOUTH
	1♣*	No	3NT**
No	4♣***	No	4♡
No	6♡	All pass	

*16+ points, any shape
** 12-13 points, 4-3-3-3 pattern
***Asking for four-card suit

The play:
1 West leads ♠K : six, two, **ace**
2 South leads ♠7 : three, **ruffed with the ace of hearts**, four
3 The ♣2 is led from dummy : three, jack . . .

How should West plan the defence?

61
Dealer North,
North-South vulnerable.

♠ A K 9
♥ A 7 4 3
♦ 6
♣ K Q 8 6 2

WEST	NORTH	EAST	SOUTH
	1♣	No	1♠
No	2♥	No	2NT
No	3♠	No	4♠
Double	No	No	No

♠ J 7 6 3 2
♥ K 8 6
♦ A 8 7 2
♣ 4

The play:
1 West leads ♠4 : **ace wins**, *East discards* ♦5
2 ♥3 is led from dummy : queen, **king,** nine
3 South leads ♣4 : five, **king,** three.

How should South continue?

62

♠ Q J 8 6 3
♥ A K J 6 3
♦ 5 3
♣ 5

Dealer South,
East-West vulnerable.

♠ A 10 9 7
♥ 7 2
♦ A 6
♣ A 9 8 7 4

WEST	NORTH	EAST	SOUTH
			1♠
No	4♠	All pass	

The play:
1 **West leads ♣A :** five, two, ten
2 **West leads ♦A :** three, two, seven.

How should West continue?

59. Better than the best?

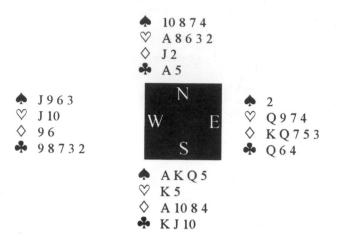

```
                    ♠  10 8 7 4
                    ♡  A 8 6 3 2
                    ◊  J 2
                    ♣  A 5

    ♠  J 9 6 3           N              ♠  2
    ♡  J 10                              ♡  Q 9 7 4
    ◊  9 6          W         E          ◊  K Q 7 5 3
    ♣  9 8 7 3 2         S              ♣  Q 6 4

                    ♠  A K Q 5
                    ♡  K 5
                    ◊  A 10 8 4
                    ♣  K J 10
```

The best start is a club finesse. Whether the club finesse works or not, you discard a diamond from dummy and plan to ruff three diamonds. If the club finesse loses, you will need some luck on the latter rounds of diamonds. You must hope that no over-ruff is available to the defenders.

The alternative line of setting up the hearts is less attractive. Even if hearts are 3-3, you have a diamond loser and if the more common 4-2 split exists, you are very likely to lose a trump as well as a diamond.

As you need entries to your hand for the diamond ruffs, you should win the first heart in dummy. As you have no inkling which way to finesse in clubs, you may as well cash the ♣A, followed by a club to your jack. When this holds, cash the ♣K, discarding a diamond from dummy. Now ◊A, diamond ruff, heart to the king and another diamond.

On the actual deal, West is helpless. If he ruffs with the ♠J and exits with a trump, dummy wins with the ♠7, a heart is ruffed high in hand and another diamond ruff sees declarer home. If West fails to ruff, you ruff with the ♠7, come to hand with a trump and lead your last diamond. No matter what West does, you have twelve tricks.

In the 1983 Bermuda Bowl semi-finals, three declarers played in slam but none came to twelve tricks. If you made this slam, you have outplayed three of the world's best players.

60. When the time is ripe

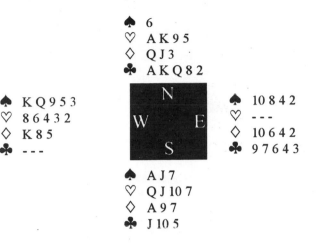

```
              ♠ 6
              ♡ A K 9 5
              ◇ Q J 3
              ♣ A K Q 8 2
♠ K Q 9 5 3        N        ♠ 10 8 4 2
♡ 8 6 4 3 2    W       E    ♡ - - -
◇ K 8 5                     ◇ 10 6 4 2
♣ - - -            S        ♣ 9 7 6 4 3
              ♠ A J 7
              ♡ Q J 10 7
              ◇ A 9 7
              ♣ J 10 5
```

This hand should be easy to defend because the South hand is an open book. The declarer is known to have started with a 3-4-3-3 pattern with every missing high card except perhaps for the jack of spades.

If East had the ten of clubs, it would be a sufficient defence for West to ruff the jack of clubs and exit with the queen of spades or a trump. On the actual deal this would allow declarer to make in comfort. The heart return would be won in hand, the jack of spades ruffed high in dummy, trumps would be drawn and declarer could claim the rest.

There is no need for West to bank on partner having the ten of clubs. The contract can be defeated for certain by refusing to ruff clubs until the third round, thus cutting declarer off from dummy. After drawing trumps, South will have no way of returning to the table to cash the remaining clubs. Declarer will have to fall back on the losing diamond finesse. As it happens, since West has the king of diamonds, the contract can still be defeated by waiting until the fourth round of clubs before ruffing, followed by a trump exit.

61. Wrong place at the right time

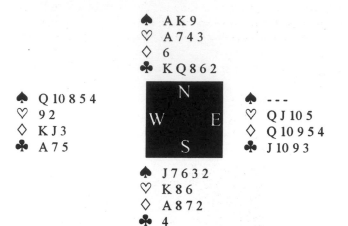

```
              ♠ A K 9
              ♥ A 7 4 3
              ◇ 6
              ♣ K Q 8 6 2
                    N
♠ Q 10 8 5 4                    ♠ - - -
♥ 9 2          W       E        ♥ Q J 10 5
◇ K J 3                         ◇ Q 10 9 5 4
♣ A 7 5             S           ♣ J 10 9 3
              ♠ J 7 6 3 2
              ♥ K 8 6
              ◇ A 8 7 2
              ♣ 4
```

At the table declarer failed as follows. A club was ruffed at trick four
followed by a heart to the ace and another club ruff, dropping the ace.
The ace of diamonds was cashed and a diamond ruff led to this ending :

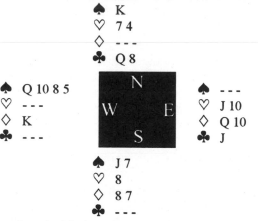

```
              ♠ K
              ♥ 7 4
              ◇ - - -
              ♣ Q 8
                    N
♠ Q 10 8 5                      ♠ - - -
♥ - - -        W       E        ♥ J 10
◇ K                             ◇ Q 10
♣ - - -             S           ♣ J
              ♠ J 7
              ♥ 8
              ◇ 8 7
              ♣ - - -
```

South continued with the queen of clubs from dummy, discarding the
heart loser. West ruffed and led a trump and nothing could prevent West
from making the last three tricks.

This was simply a case of mistiming. South needs to ruff not one but two
diamonds in dummy. After a heart to the ace at trick five, continue with
a diamond to the ace, a diamond ruff and a club ruff.

The five-card ending is the same except that the lead is in the South hand. South ruffs a diamond with the king of spades and leads any card from dummy, playing the losing heart from hand. West, trump-bound, has to ruff and give declarer the tenth trick with the jack of spades.

62. Early recognition

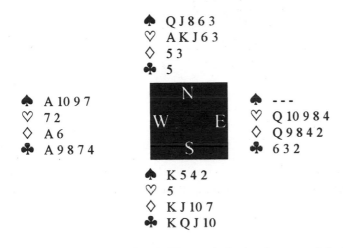

```
              ♠  Q J 8 6 3
              ♡  A K J 6 3
              ◇  5 3
              ♣  5

♠  A 10 9 7                      ♠  - - -
♡  7 2                           ♡  Q 10 9 8 4
◇  A 6                           ◇  Q 9 8 4 2
♣  A 9 8 7 4                     ♣  6 3 2

              ♠  K 5 4 2
              ♡  5
              ◇  K J 10 7
              ♣  K Q J 10
```

In the 1970 Bermuda Bowl, West switched to hearts and declarer made the contract. The ace of hearts won and the three of spades went to the king and ace. South won the diamond return and cashed two clubs, throwing hearts from dummy. A spade to the ten and jack was followed by the heart jack, ruffed by South, and a further spade finesse.

West failed to recognise the problem in time. The game could be beaten if South could be prevented from returning to hand twice *after* learning of the 4-0 trump split. The only entry in the South hand that can be attacked is in diamonds. Therefore lead another diamond at trick three.

South wins and plays the king of spades. West takes the ace and exits with a heart. South can ruff the next heart to hand, cash two clubs, as before, but when a spade is led, West inserts the nine or ten. Stuck in dummy, South has to concede a second trump trick to West.

63

Teams, dealer West,
East-West vulnerable.

	♠	10 7 5 4
	♡	K 9 8
	♢	10 3 2
	♣	K J 9

WEST	NORTH	EAST	SOUTH
No	No	No	2NT
No	3♣*	No	3NT**
No	No	No	

```
        N
    W       E
        S
```

*5-card major Stayman
**No 5-card major,
no 4-card major

	♠	A K J
	♡	J 4
	♢	A K J 5
	♣	A 10 4 2

The play:

Against strong defenders, the play goes:

1 West leads ♡2: eight, **queen,** four
2 East returns ♡6: jack, **ace,** nine
3 West plays ♡5: **king,** three . . .

What should South discard? Plan the play for South.

64

	♠	2
	♡	10 8 4
	♢	A 10 3 2
	♣	Q J 9 6 2

Teams, dealer North,
North-South vulnerable.

♠	10 9 8 3
♡	A K Q 7 2
♢	J 6
♣	8 4

```
        N
    W       E
        S
```

WEST	NORTH	EAST	SOUTH
	No	4♢	4♠
No	No	No	

The play:

1 **West leads ♡K:** four, six, five
2 **West leads ♡Q:** eight, three, nine
3 **West leads ♡A:** *East discards the ♢9.*

How should West continue?

65
Teams, dealer South,
North-South vulnerable.

♠ J 10 2
♡ K 9 8
◇ 8 6 3
♣ 9 7 6 2

WEST	NORTH	EAST	SOUTH
			1♠
2♡	No	4♡	4♠
No	No	Dble	End

♠ A K 9 8 6 4
♡ 6
◇ A Q J 7 2
♣ 4

The play:
1 **West leads ♣K:** two, five, four
2 **West switches to ♡Q:** eight, seven, six
3 West leads ♡J: nine, three, *ruffed with ♠4.*

How should South continue?

66
Teams, dealer South,
neither side vulnerable.

♠ A 9 3
♡ A K 7 6 5 4
◇ 9 8 3
♣ 6

WEST	NORTH	EAST	SOUTH
			3◇
5♣	5◇	All pass	

♠ J 10 7 6
♡ Q J 10 9 8
◇ 10
♣ A 7 3

The play :
1 West leads ♡3: **ace,** eight, two
2 ◇3 is led from dummy: ten, queen, **ace**
3 West plays ♣10: six, **ace,** eight.

How should East continue?

63. Home is where the heart is

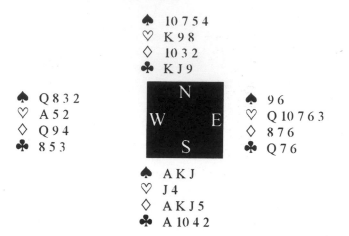

```
               ♠  10 7 5 4
               ♡  K 9 8
               ◊  10 3 2
               ♣  K J 9

♠ Q 8 3 2          N          ♠  9 6
♡ A 5 2                       ♡  Q 10 7 6 3
◊ Q 9 4      W         E      ◊  8 7 6
♣ 8 5 3            S          ♣  Q 7 6

               ♠  A K J
               ♡  J 4
               ◊  A K J 5
               ♣  A 10 4 2
```

In practice the declarer failed. Placing the long hearts with West, South took the club finesse into the 'safe' hand. East cashed two more hearts for one down.

East's play in hearts (Q-then-6-then-3) is not consistent with a four-card holding, but tallies with either a three-card or a five-card suit. The clue to the location of the heart length lies in the second trick. Had West started with five hearts (and led the *two* of hearts as a false card), the expert defence would be to duck the second round of hearts in order to keep communication with East. The failure to duck marks West, given to be a strong defender, with the shorter heart holding. As West does not have five hearts and East does not have four, the actual position can be pin-pointed.

South should discard the jack of spades on the third heart, cash the king of clubs and then run the nine. If the nine of clubs loses to the queen, the jack of clubs provides an entry to take the diamond finesse into the safe hand. If the nine of clubs holds, South should switch to diamonds and finesse the jack. To repeat the club finesse could be expensive if West has held off with the queen, for there would now be no entry left in dummy for the diamond finesse.

64. Trusting partner

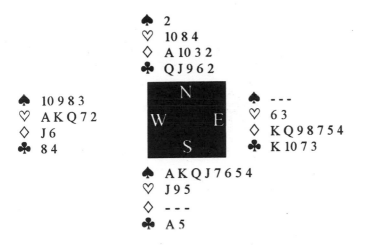

```
              ♠  2
              ♡  10 8 4
              ◇  A 10 3 2
              ♣  Q J 9 6 2

♠  10 9 8 3                      ♠  - - -
♡  A K Q 7 2                     ♡  6 3
◇  J 6                           ◇  K Q 9 8 7 5 4
♣  8 4                           ♣  K 10 7 3

              ♠  A K Q J 7 6 5 4
              ♡  J 9 5
              ◇  - - -
              ♣  A 5
```

The only continuation to defeat the contract is a trump. How can West deduce that?

The solution calls for a high degree of partnership cooperation and trust. Missing the ace, jack and ten of diamonds, East must surely have a seven-card suit to justify that opening bid of four diamonds. In that case East must know that the defence cannot come to a diamond trick. Why then signal with the *nine* of diamonds, asking for a diamond switch?

At the time of the discard East did not know, of course, whether West began with four hearts or five. If there were a possibility of over-ruffing dummy (in the situation where West began with A-K-Q-x in hearts and South with J-x-x-x) East would discourage diamonds.

But East did not discourage diamonds. Therefore East cannot over-ruff dummy and so East must be void in trumps. South must therefore have started with eight spades, three hearts and two clubs. West can deduce that only a trump lead can strand declarer in hand.

65. Enter once, enter twice

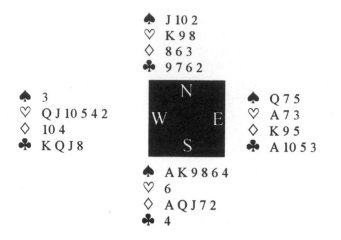

```
                    ♠ J 10 2
                    ♡ K 9 8
                    ◇ 8 6 3
                    ♣ 9 7 6 2

♠ 3                                      ♠ Q 7 5
♡ Q J 10 5 4 2          N                ♡ A 7 3
◇ 10 4             W         E           ◇ K 9 5
♣ K Q J 8               S                ♣ A 10 5 3

                    ♠ A K 9 8 6 4
                    ♡ 6
                    ◇ A Q J 7 2
                    ♣ 4
```

The winning play, not found at the table in an international tournament, is to lead the eight or nine of spades at trick four and play low in dummy. East is faced with a dilemma. If the queen of spades wins, there are two entries in dummy to take and repeat the diamond finesse. If East does not take the queen of spades, declarer draws trumps without loss and concedes a trick to the king of diamonds.

The competing plays are inferior : (1) Play off ace and king of spades, hoping for the queen to drop. This is unlikely in view of East's double. (2) Play a low spade to the jack, or a top spade followed by a low spade to the jack. This provides only one entry to dummy and success will require the king of diamonds to be doubleton with East.

If it turns out that East began with all four missing trumps, the recommended line is still best. If East takes the queen of spades on the first round, you have your two entries. If East correctly ducks, you can continue with a low spade to the jack and hope that East has king doubleton in diamonds.

A fringe benefit of leading the eight or nine of spades occurs when West has Q-x-x in spades, though this is unlikely. West may well duck for fear of colliding with East's singleton king or ace in spades.

66. No hurry to help yourself

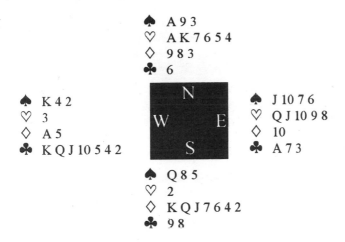

```
              ♠ A 9 3
              ♡ A K 7 6 5 4
              ◇ 9 8 3
              ♣ 6
  ♠ K 4 2            N            ♠ J 10 7 6
  ♡ 3        W              E     ♡ Q J 10 9 8
  ◇ A 5                           ◇ 10
  ♣ K Q J 10 5 4 2    S          ♣ A 7 3
              ♠ Q 8 5
              ♡ 2
              ◇ K Q J 7 6 4 2
              ♣ 9 8
```

In practice East continued with a heart, hoping that South would discard
or that West would be able to over-ruff. This turned out to be futile.
South ruffed high, played a low trump to dummy (drawing West's last
trump), ruffed another heart, ruffed a club and ruffed a third heart.
A spade to dummy's ace allowed South to discard the spade losers on the
king of hearts and the established seven of hearts.

Had East returned a club or the jack of spades, the contract would have
failed since dummy would have been one entry short to set up and cash
the sixth heart. East could not blame partner for leading the ten of clubs.
West was not to know that the declarer had also started with a singleton
heart. In any event East could be almost certain that the ten of clubs was
a false card.

East's defence would have worked if West's diamonds had been as good
as A-J doubleton. This possibility was a little remote compared with the
likelihood that the heart return would help declarer set up the heart suit.

67
Teams. dealer East.
East-West vulnerable.

♠ A K Q 3
♥ A K 7
♦ 9 7
♣ A 8 5 4

WEST	NORTH	EAST	SOUTH
		1♦	No
No	Double	No	1♠
No	3♠	No	4♠
No	No	No	

♠ 10 8 5 4
♥ 10 6 4 2
♦ J 8 6 5 3
♣ - - -

The play:
1 **West leads ♦K:** seven. four. three
2 West plays ♦10: nine, **queen,** five
3 East continues with ♦2: six. *West ruffs with the ♠9* . . .

Plan South's play.

68

♠ A 10 8 5 4
♥ A Q 10
♦ 7 5
♣ 8 7 5

Teams. dealer East
North-South vulnerable.

♠ 9 6
♥ K 9 8 3
♦ 10 9 4 3
♣ A J 4

WEST	NORTH	EAST	SOUTH
		No	2♣*
No	2♦*	No	2NT*
No	3♠	No	3NT
No	No	No	

*2♣ = Precision, 11-15 points 5+ clubs: 2♦ = artificial relay: 2NT = maximum opening, no second suit

The play:
1 West leads ♦3 : five, **queen,** two
2 East returns ♦K: **ace,** four, seven
3 **South plays ♣K:** four, five, three
4 South plays ♠J: six, **ace,** three
5 ♣8 is led from dummy: *East discards ♥4,* ten, **jack.**

How should West continue?

69

Teams, dealer West,
neither side vulnerable.

♠ Q 9
♡ J 8 6 3
♢ Q J 10
♣ K J 8 4

WEST	NORTH	EAST	SOUTH
1♢	No	2♢	4♠
No	No	No	

Both pairs are using a
12-14 1NT opening.

♠ K J 7 6 5 4 3
♡ A K Q 9
♢ 7
♣ 2

The play:
1 West leads ♢2: **East wins the ace**
2 East returns ♡2: **South wins the ace,** West plays the five.

Plan South's play.

70

Rubber, dealer North,
East-West vulnerable.

♠ 4 2
♡ Q J 10 5 3
♢ 8 6
♣ A K 5 4

WEST	NORTH	EAST	SOUTH
	1♡*	No	2♢
No	2♡	No	2♠
No	2NT	No	5♢
No	No	No	

♠ A K
♡ A 7 6 4 2
♢ J 9 3
♣ 9 7 2

*Still filled with the zest for life

The play:
1 West leads ♣3: four, nine, **queen**
2 South leads ♠5: three, two, **king**
3 East leads ♢3: **ace,** four, six
4 South plays ♠6: seven, four, **ace.**

How should East continue?

67. With a world title at stake

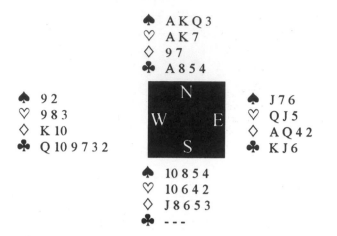

```
                    ♠ A K Q 3
                    ♡ A K 7
                    ◇ 9 7
                    ♣ A 8 5 4
♠ 9 2                                    ♠ J 7 6
♡ 9 8 3                                  ♡ Q J 5
◇ K 10                                   ◇ A Q 4 2
♣ Q 10 9 7 3 2                           ♣ K J 6
                    ♠ 10 8 5 4
                    ♡ 10 6 4 2
                    ◇ J 8 6 5 3
                    ♣ - - -
```

In the final of the 1983 Bermuda Bowl, won by the USA by 5 Imps, the Italian declarer failed to make 4♠. Had he succeeded, Italy would have won the world crown.

After ◇K, diamond to the queen, followed by a low diamond from East, ruffed by West with the ♠9, declarer over-ruffed with dummy's ♠Q. This created a trump trick for East. Next came ♣A, club ruff, heart to the ace, club ruff, heart to the king and the last club from dummy. East pitched the ◇A and declarer ruffed. He now led a diamond, West ruffed with the ♠2 and declarer discarded the heart loser from dummy. As East had a trump trick to come, that was one down.

While there is a winning line double-dummy by over-ruffing West on the third diamond, there is a much easier solution. Do not over-ruff but discard dummy's heart loser instead. Declarer is in control and simply needs to ruff three clubs in hand. If West exits with a trump, dummy wins and the play goes: low club ruffed, heart to the king, low club ruffed, heart to the ace, the third low club ruffed in hand.

At this point only two trumps are held by the opponents and East has not had a chance to discard a diamond. It is therefore safe to lead a diamond, ruffing in dummy, and draw the missing trumps.

68. Cut him off

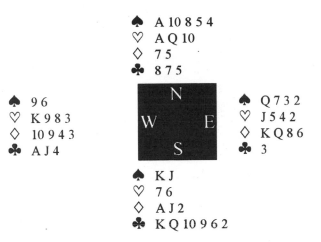

```
              ♠ A 10 8 5 4
              ♥ A Q 10
              ◇ 7 5
              ♣ 8 7 5

♠ 9 6                           ♠ Q 7 3 2
♥ K 9 8 3          N            ♥ J 5 4 2
◇ 10 9 4 3     W       E        ◇ K Q 8 6
♣ A J 4            S            ♣ 3

              ♠ K J
              ♥ 7 6
              ◇ A J 2
              ♣ K Q 10 9 6 2
```

West should return the nine of spades, taking out South's entry to the clubs before the suit can be established.

South is known to have started with the king and queen of clubs, the ace and jack of diamonds (East played the *queen* of diamonds at trick one, thereby denying the jack) and the jack of spades. To qualify as a maximum opener, South must hold the king of spades as well. However, the failure to raise spades means South will not hold a third spade.

Note that South makes 3NT in comfort if West returns a diamond or a heart. On a spade return, South can do no better than take the heart finesse and set up the spades, making four spades, two hearts, one diamond and one club. East naturally has to cooperate by withholding the queen of spades on the second round, and by returning the jack of hearts or the fourth spade when in with the queen of spades.

It does South no good to cash the jack of diamonds after winning with the king of spades. The defence can then cash out their five tricks when East takes the queen of spades.

South should, of course, have played a second club from hand at trick four without touching the spades.

69. Putting it all together

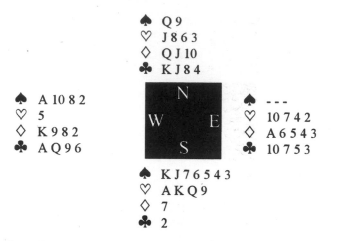

```
              ♠ Q 9
              ♡ J 8 6 3
              ◇ Q J 10
              ♣ K J 8 4
♠ A 10 8 2              ♠ - - -
♡ 5              N       ♡ 10 7 4 2
◇ K 9 8 2   W       E   ◇ A 6 5 4 3
♣ A Q 9 6       S       ♣ 10 7 5 3
              ♠ K J 7 6 5 4 3
              ♡ A K Q 9
              ◇ 7
              ♣ 2
```

Once East has shown up with the ace of diamonds, the remaining high cards can be placed with West who opened the bidding. These are the ace of spades, the king of diamonds and the ace and queen of clubs.

Why did West not open with a bid of 1NT with this collection of thirteen points? Clearly because the hand was unbalanced.

Why then open one diamond on what appears from the opening lead of the *two* of diamonds to be a four-card suit? Because West has no suit longer than four cards. Having an unbalanced hand with only four-card suits, West must have a 4-4-4-1 pattern.

When you lead a spade, if West plays low you must finesse the nine to avoid two trump losers. If West started with

♠ A ♡ 10 7 5 4 ◇ K 9 8 2 ♣ A Q 9 6

and the defence scores a heart ruff, console yourself with the thought that you could not have prevented it.

On the actual deal, West could have beaten you by leading the singleton but you need concern yourself only with the defence produced at the table. The point is to avoid the automatic, mechanical, unquestioning play of a spade to the queen at trick three. Not everyone will agree with you that the contract failed because of bad luck.

70. Severing the connection

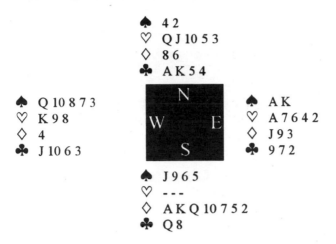

```
                        ♠ 4 2
                        ♡ Q J 10 5 3
                        ◇ 8 6
                        ♣ A K 5 4
 ♠ Q 10 8 7 3          N            ♠ A K
 ♡ K 9 8          W         E       ♡ A 7 6 4 2
 ◇ 4                                ◇ J 9 3
 ♣ J 10 6 3            S            ♣ 9 7 2
                        ♠ J 9 6 5
                        ♡ - - -
                        ◇ A K Q 10 7 5 2
                        ♣ Q 8
```

East must return a club at trick five to defeat the contract. South is known to have started with two clubs (West led the *three* of clubs, indicating a maximum of four clubs as East has the two), four spades (the suit would have been rebid with five) and six or seven diamonds. It is almost certain that South began with seven diamonds, for with a singleton heart, declarer would have lost no time in discarding it on the third round of clubs.

In fact East could have solved any problems by playing the ace of hearts or a club at trick three. The diamond return was unnecessary since East can always over-ruff dummy.

A diamond or a heart return at trick five allows declarer to make the contract by a squeeze on West in the black suits. The play of the diamonds will reduce West to ♠ Q and ♣ J-10-6 while dummy has the ♡Q ♣ A-K-5 and South has ♠J-9 ◇2 ♣8. When South leads the two of diamonds, West must unguard one of the black suits and declarer makes the rest.

The club return breaks up the squeeze by cutting off the declarer from the club menace in dummy.

71

Rubber, dealer West,
neither side vulnerable.

♠ A K Q 10 4 3
♥ A 6 3
♦ 7 4
♣ Q 7

WEST	NORTH	EAST	SOUTH
3 ◊	3 ♠	No	3NT
No	No	No	

```
        N
    W       E
        S
```

♠ 6
♥ 9 7 4 2
♦ A K 5
♣ A 9 6 4 3

The play:

West leads the king of hearts. Plan South's play.

(If South ducks in dummy, West continues with the queen of hearts and then the jack of hearts, East following suit each time.)

72

♠ A 5 4 3 2
♥ J
♦ K Q 8 7 4
♣ Q 4

Teams, dealer West,
neither side vulnerable.

♠ K J 10 6
♥ K 8 3
♦ 5 3 2
♣ K 7 5

```
        N
    W       E
        S
```

WEST	NORTH	EAST	SOUTH
No	1 ♠	No	2 ♣
No	2 ◊	No	2NT*
No	3 ◊	No	3NT
No	No	No	

*Not forcing

The play:

1 West leads ♥3: jack, queen, **ace**
2 **South leads ◊J:** two, four, six
3 South leads ◊10: five, seven, **ace**
4 East returns ♥5: ten, **king,** *dummy discards ♠2.*

How should West continue?

73
Dealer South,
North-South vulnerable.

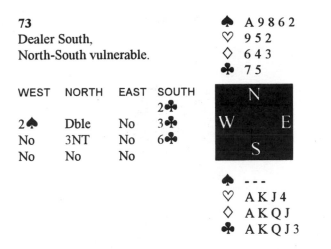

	♠	A 9 8 6 2
	♡	9 5 2
	◇	6 4 3
	♣	7 5

WEST	NORTH	EAST	SOUTH
			2♣
2♠	Dble	No	3♣
No	3NT	No	6♣
No	No	No	

♠ - - -
♡ A K J 4
◇ A K Q J
♣ A K Q J 3

West leads the ten of diamonds, won by the ace. The trumps turn out to be 3-3, and West discards a spade on the third diamond.

How should South play?

74

	♠	J 10 9
	♡	K Q J 4
	◇	J 3
	♣	K 5 4 3

Dealer South
both sides vulnerable.

♠ K Q 5 3
♡ 8
◇ K 9 5
♣ Q 9 8 7 2

WEST	NORTH	EAST	SOUTH
			1◇
No	1♡	No	1NT*
No	3NT	All pass	
*15-16 points			

The play:
1 West leads ♣7 : three, *East discards ♡2*, **jack**
2 South leads ♡7: eight, **king**, five
3 ◇J is led from dummy: **ace,** two, five
4 East leads ♠6: seven, **queen**, nine.

How should West continue?

71. Counter move

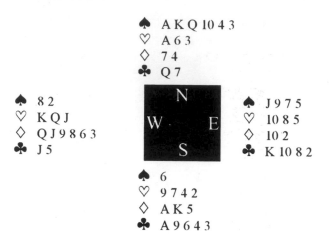

```
                    ♠  A K Q 10 4 3
                    ♡  A 6 3
                    ◇  7 4
                    ♣  Q 7

    ♠  8 2              N              ♠  J 9 7 5
    ♡  K Q J                           ♡  10 8 5
    ◇  Q J 9 8 6 3   W       E         ◇  10 2
    ♣  J 5                             ♣  K 10 8 2
                       S
                    ♠  6
                    ♡  9 7 4 2
                    ◇  A K 5
                    ♣  A 9 6 4 3
```

South should not expect the spades to break evenly. It is therefore worthwhile to hold up the ace of hearts in an attempt to preserve an entry for the spades.

The defence does best by continuing hearts to knock out the entry. If declarer takes the first or second heart, the contract can be defeated.

Once West, who opened three diamonds, has shown up with the king, queen and jack of hearts, declarer can be confident that the king of clubs will be with East. After winning the third round of hearts, cash the ace and king of diamonds, eliminating East's holding in that suit, followed by your fourth heart, discarding a spade from dummy. Then play the spades from the top down. On winning the fourth spade, East will be forced to lead away from the king of clubs.

On the actual deal, this line produces ten tricks. If East happened to have five spades, the endplay in clubs gives declarer the ninth trick.

72. No entry, no future

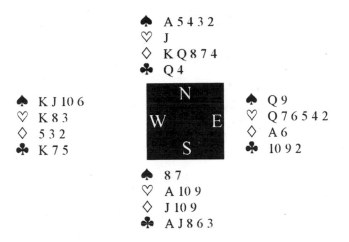

```
              ♠ A 5 4 3 2
              ♡ J
              ◇ K Q 8 7 4
              ♣ Q 4
  ♠ K J 10 6              ♠ Q 9
  ♡ K 8 3                 ♡ Q 7 6 5 4 2
  ◇ 5 3 2                 ◇ A 6
  ♣ K 7 5                 ♣ 10 9 2
              ♠ 8 7
              ♡ A 10 9
              ◇ J 10 9
              ♣ A J 8 6 3
```

South's 2♣ followed by 2NT non-forcing indicates 10-12 points. So far, South has shown up with the ♡A and the ◇J, and East with ♡Q and ◇A. The missing points are the ♠Q, ♣A and ♣J. Of these, South has to hold the ♣A and at least one other black honour to justify the bidding.

After trick 4, South has seven tricks available, four in diamonds plus three aces. It is tempting and instinctive to play a third heart to set up East's heart suit, but with the ♣A marked with declarer, East cannot have a quick entry to cash the hearts.

As you have an entry with the ♣K, you should set up winners in your hand rather than in partner's. Switch to the ♠K at trick 5. If South began with ♠Q-x, that still gives South only eight tricks and you can revert to hearts (hoping East began with at least ♡Q-9-7-x-x) after you come in with the ♣K. A lower spade would work here but the ♠K is better in case South holds ♠Q singleton. Note that on a heart return, South wins and can make nine tricks easily.

In the 1983 Bermuda Bowl semi-finals, Peter Weichsel (USA) switched to the ♠K at trick 5 and defeated the contract. At the other table, 3◇ was passed out and made ten tricks.

117

73. Let them do your work for you

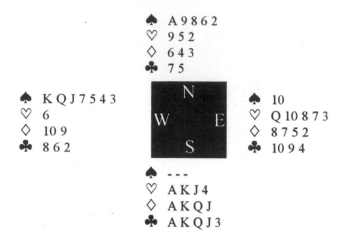

```
                    ♠  A 9 8 6 2
                    ♡  9 5 2
                    ◇  6 4 3
                    ♣  7 5
♠  K Q J 7 5 4 3        N           ♠  10
♡  6                               ♡  Q 10 8 7 3
◇  10 9            W       E        ◇  8 7 5 2
♣  8 6 2              S             ♣  10 9 4
                    ♠  - - -
                    ♡  A K J 4
                    ◇  A K Q J
                    ♣  A K Q J 3
```

South should play off the fourth diamond, discarding a spade from dummy. Then cash the ace of hearts and exit with the four of hearts.

In most positions the defenders will be end-played. A spade return will concede the contract at once while a heart return by West will run into South's tenace. On this line of play the slam is bound to make whenever
(a) West has the ten of hearts, with or without the queen,
(b) either defender has a doubleton honour, or
(c) either defender has a singleton or a void in hearts.

A problem will arise only when East has 10-x-x or Q-10-x-x. Then East will win with the ten and return a low heart. Declarer will now have to make the right guess to land the slam.

West has turned up with three clubs and two diamonds and is likely to hold six spades for the 2♠ bid over 2♣. It is therefore preferable to play West to have started with two low hearts than with ♡Q-x-x.

Once West has followed to the second diamond and you have played off your diamond winners, it is quite safe to cash your last two trumps (discarding spades from dummy) before playing ace of hearts followed by a low heart. A defender may unwisely discard a heart on the trumps.

118

74. Bouquets all round?

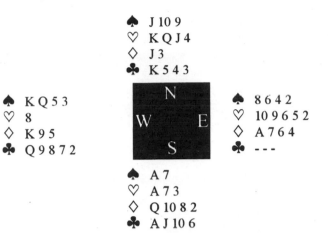

```
                    ♠ J 10 9
                    ♡ K Q J 4
                    ◇ J 3
                    ♣ K 5 4 3
   ♠ K Q 5 3          N          ♠ 8 6 4 2
   ♡ 8           W         E     ♡ 10 9 6 5 2
   ◇ K 9 5                       ◇ A 7 6 4
   ♣ Q 9 8 7 2        S          ♣ - - -
                    ♠ A 7
                    ♡ A 7 3
                    ◇ Q 10 8 2
                    ♣ A J 10 6
```

West must continue with a low spade, dropping South's doubleton ace.
The defenders can then make three spades and two diamonds before
declarer can come to nine tricks via the diamonds.

It should not be too hard for West to find this play. Staring at ten points
in hand and eleven in dummy, and South marked with at least fifteen for
the one no-trump rebid, West can deduce that East cannot have more in
high cards than the ace of diamonds already seen. South has four heart
tricks, three clubs and the ace of spades. Given time, declarer will
establish a ninth trick in diamonds. South would not have led the jack of
diamonds from dummy unless holding the ten as well as the queen.

West cannot be sure the ace of spades is doubleton, but can be sure that
there is no other chance. Necessity is the mother of accurate defence.

Bouquets are due to both declarer and partner: to South for crossing to
dummy to lead a diamond rather than leading the suit from hand, and to
East for rising with the ace of diamonds. If East plays low on the jack of
diamonds, the contract cannot be defeated.

And so, are there also bouquets due to you as West?

75
Dealer South,
both sides vulnerable.

♠ J 6
♡ A K 9 4
◇ A 6 3 2
♣ 5 4 2

WEST	NORTH	EAST	SOUTH
			1NT
No	2♣	No	2♡
No	4♡	All pass	

♠ A 8 3
♡ 10 6 3 2
◇ K 7
♣ A Q 10 8

The play:
1 West leads ◇10: **dummy's ace wins**
2 ♣2 is led from dummy: nine, ten, **king**
3 West leads ◇Q: **king wins**
4 South leads ♡2: seven, **ace,** five
5 ♣4 is led from dummy: jack, **ace,** three.

How should South continue?

76
Dealer West,
neither side vulnerable.

♠ K Q
♡ A K 6 4
◇ K 8 6
♣ K Q 9 7

WEST	NORTH	EAST	SOUTH
No	1♣	1◇	1♠
No	2NT*	No	4♠
No	No	No	

*19-20, balanced

♠ A J 4 2
♡ 7
◇ A J 10 7 3 2
♣ 6 2

The play:
1 West leads ◇9: six, ten, **queen**
2 South plays ♠3: seven, king, **ace.**

How should East continue?

77
Teams, dealer East,
North-South vulnerable.

♠ 9 8 6 2
♡ A 10 5 4
♢ 10 6 3
♣ A 5

WEST	NORTH	EAST	SOUTH
		1♡	2♢
5♣*	5♢	All pass	

♠ J 7 4
♡ K 3 2
♢ A K Q 9 8 4 2
♣ - - -

The play:
1 West leads the jack of hearts . . .

Having been lucky to escape a spade lead, how should South play?

78
Teams, dealer South,
neither side vulnerable.

♠ Q 6 5
♡ 8 3 2
♢ 10 7 5 4
♣ J 10 5

WEST	NORTH	EAST	SOUTH
			2♣
No	2♢	No	2NT*
No	3NT	All pass	

*23-24 balanced, not forcing

♠ A K 7 2
♡ 9 6 4
♢ K
♣ 8 7 6 4 2

The play:
1 West leads ♡5: two, four, **king**
2 **South plays ♢A:** two, four, king
3 South plays ♢8: **queen,** five, *East discards ♣2*
4 West leads ♠J: queen, **king,** four.

How should East continue, with the *ace* of spades or the *two* of spades?

The solution is a matter of logic, not guesswork. No merit for answers
unsupported by reasons.

79
Teams, dealer North,
neither side vulnerable.

♠ 8 4
♥ A 6 5 4
♦ A 3 2
♣ 10 4 3 2

WEST	NORTH	EAST	SOUTH
	No	No	1♠
No	1NT	No	2♥
No	3♥	All pass	

♠ K Q 6 5 3
♥ K J 10 8
♦ 6 5
♣ Q J

The play:
1 **West leads ♣A:** two, five, jack
2 West switches to ♦J: **ace,** eight, five
3 The ♠4 is led from dummy: two, **king,** seven
4 ♠3 from hand: nine, eight, **jack**
5 ♦**K from East:** six, four, two
6 ♦Q from East: *ruffed with* ♥*8,* nine, three
7 ♠5 from hand: ten, *ruffed with* ♥*4,* ace of spades

How should South continue?

80
Dealer South,
East-West vulnerable.

♠ A K 4
♥ 10 8 4
♦ 9 6
♣ A J 10 9 3

WEST	NORTH	EAST	SOUTH
			1♥
No	2♣	No	2NT*
No	3.♥	No	4♥
No	No	No	
*15-17			

♠ 7 6 3
♥ Q J 3 2
♦ A K 4 2
♣ 5 2

West leads the queen of diamonds. Plan East's defence.

75. Keeping control at all times

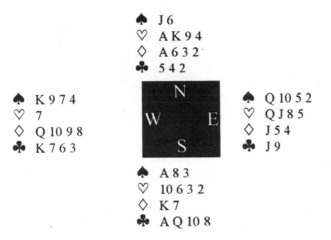

```
                    ♠  J 6
                    ♡  A K 9 4
                    ◇  A 6 3 2
                    ♣  5 4 2
  ♠  K 9 7 4                        ♠  Q 10 5 2
  ♡  7              N               ♡  Q J 8 5
  ◇  Q 10 9 8   W       E           ◇  J 5 4
  ♣  K 7 6 3        S               ♣  J 9
                    ♠  A 8 3
                    ♡  10 6 3 2
                    ◇  K 7
                    ♣  A Q 10 8
```

At the table South continued with a second trump, a seemingly innocuous play, but when East turned up with Q-J-x-x in trumps, the contract could no longer be made. East ruffed the third club and drew a third round of trumps, leaving South with only nine tricks.

South should foresee the danger of a 4-1 trump break and should continue clubs at trick six. East may ruff and return a trump, but the declarer is in full control, making ten tricks on cross-ruff lines.

There is no danger when trumps are 3-2, even if the third club is ruffed by the short trump hand. Declarer wins the return, draws a second round of trumps and proceeds with the cross-ruff, losing at most two trumps and the king of clubs.

76. Oh, what a tangled web

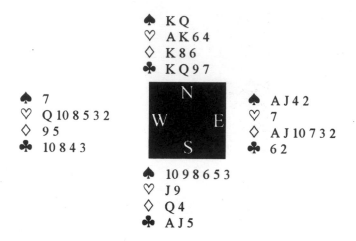

```
              ♠ K Q
              ♡ A K 6 4
              ◇ K 8 6
              ♣ K Q 9 7
                      N
♠ 7                               ♠ A J 4 2
♡ Q 10 8 5 3 2    W       E       ♡ 7
◇ 9 5                             ◇ A J 10 7 3 2
♣ 10 8 4 3            S           ♣ 6 2
              ♠ 10 9 8 6 5 3
              ♡ J 9
              ◇ Q 4
              ♣ A J 5
```

The best return at trick three is the two of clubs, the play East would make with a singleton club. South is marked with six spades for the jump to game and so to try to give West a diamond ruff is futile. But see what may happen if South believes you have a singleton club.

South wins the club, plays a spade to the queen and receives the bad news. At this point, in order to guard against fraud, it is best to cash one top heart and then play the king of diamonds to prepare a safe way back to hand. However, many a declarer may overlook the precaution of cashing a high heart and just exit with the king of diamonds. If that happens, you have a good chance to defeat the contract. Take the ace of diamonds and continue with the jack of diamonds. South will ruff and lead the ten of spades to your jack. Now play the seven of hearts and declarer will be stranded in dummy, wondering whether to return to hand with a club or with a third-round heart ruff. If South misguesses and continues hearts (as is likely), your ruff is the setting trick.

It is worth noting that this deception would have had no chance if you had played ace and another diamond at tricks one and two. Declarer would later have discarded a heart on the king of diamonds, thus preparing a safe way of returning to hand.

77. Hope for the best

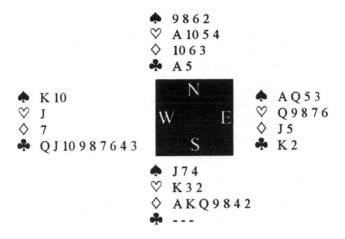

♠ 9 8 6 2
♡ A 10 5 4
◇ 10 6 3
♣ A 5

♠ K 10
♡ J
◇ 7
♣ Q J 10 9 8 7 6 4 3

N
W E
S

♠ A Q 5 3
♡ Q 9 8 7 6
◇ J 5
♣ K 2

♠ J 7 4
♡ K 3 2
◇ A K Q 9 8 4 2
♣ - - -

No doubt North should have doubled five clubs (although the defenders
have to cash their tricks very precisely to beat that contract), but you
need not concern yourself with what might have been.

You need something good to happen in spades. The best chance is to win
with the ace of hearts, play the ace of clubs, pitching ♠4, ruff the second
club, draw trumps (you need them to be 2-1) and then exit with a spade.

The seven of spades is the better choice as it increases the chance of
West's playing low from A-x, K-x or Q-x. You hope that after winning
the second spade the defenders will be end-played. A club will give you
a ruff and discard, while if East plays a heart, you will allow that to run
to the ten.

There are many positions where you will succeed, with spades either 3-3
or 4-2, although you may have to pick the end-position. For example, in
the above diagram when a spade is led, West can win and continue with
spades. When East overtakes and returns a low spade, you have to
decide whether East started with A-x-x or A-Q-x-x in spades — not too
difficult, perhaps, although the position is not certain. East might have
opened with

♠ A x x   ♡ Q x x x x   ◇ J x   ♣ K Q x.

78. Point count reveals shape

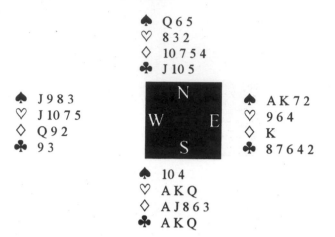

```
              ♠ Q 6 5
              ♡ 8 3 2
              ◇ 10 7 5 4
              ♣ J 10 5

♠ J 9 8 3          N          ♠ A K 7 2
♡ J 10 7 5     W       E      ♡ 9 6 4
◇ Q 9 2            S          ◇ K
♣ 9 3                         ♣ 8 7 6 4 2

              ♠ 10 4
              ♡ A K Q
              ◇ A J 8 6 3
              ♣ A K Q
```

If West began with ♠J-10-x, you must continue with the *two* of spades to avoid blocking the suit. However, if the position is as above, you must continue with the *ace* of spades to fell the ten. You cannot blame partner for making things difficult, as the *jack* of spades from West is the only card to give the defence a chance.

How can East work out which situation exists? The reasoning goes as follows : (a) West's lead of the *five* of hearts, the lowest heart indicates West began with no more than four hearts and so declarer must hold three hearts at least. (b) South's approach to the diamonds indicates a five-card holding, and this is confirmed by West's *two* of diamonds on the first round. (c) The three top hearts plus ace and jack of diamonds add up to fourteen points. Therefore South must have a further nine points in clubs (A-K-Q) to make up the quota of twenty-three required by the opening bid. It follows that South can have only two spades.

The answer is the same if we give South A-K-Q-J in hearts and remove the queen of clubs. That would give South a 2-4-5-2 pattern and again South can have only two spades.

East must therefore continue with the *ace* of spades at trick five. The hand is fascinating in that it is one of the rare cases where a defender can deduce the shape of declarer's hand by counting high card points.

79. Keep counting those points

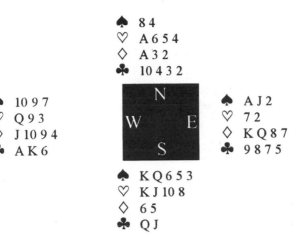

♠ 8 4
♥ A 6 5 4
♦ A 3 2
♣ 10 4 3 2

♠ 10 9 7
♥ Q 9 3
♦ J 10 9 4
♣ A K 6

♠ A J 2
♥ 7 2
♦ K Q 8 7
♣ 9 8 7 5

♠ K Q 6 5 3
♥ K J 10 8
♦ 6 5
♣ Q J

So far you have lost one spade, one diamond and one club and a second club loser is inevitable. You therefore cannot afford to lose a trick to the queen of trumps.

If you have kept a close watch, you will have noticed that East has turned up with the K-Q of diamonds and A-J of spades. That comes to 10 HCP and if East held the ♥Q as well, East would almost certainly have opened the bidding. As East passed second-in-hand, you should place the queen of hearts with West.

Having ruffed the third round of spades in dummy at trick 7, you lead a low heart to your king and continue with the jack of hearts. If the queen appears, all is plain sailing. On the actual deal, West plays low and the jack of hearts wins.

You cannot afford a third round of hearts since you have no entry back to hand, but the solution is easy. You simply lead winning spades. If West ruffs, you over-ruff in dummy and still have a trump in hand. If West declines to over-ruff you score your spade tricks and a heart, losing the last trick in clubs.

80. Put yourself in declarer's shoes

```
                    ♠ A K 4
                    ♡ 10 8 4
                    ◇ 9 6
                    ♣ A J 10 9 3
♠ 10 9 5 2              N              ♠ 7 6 3
♡ 6                                    ♡ Q J 3 2
◇ Q J 10 8       W         E           ◇ A K 4 2
♣ 8 7 6 4              S              ♣ 5 2
                    ♠ Q J 8
                    ♡ A K 9 7 5
                    ◇ 7 5 3
                    ♣ K Q
```

You hold 10 points, dummy has 12. Add the three points from partner's ◇Q implying the ◇J and you have 25 HCP. The remaining HCP must all be with declarer whose 2NT rebid showed 15-17 points.

You can score two diamond tricks plus whatever you make in trumps. As the cards lie, declarer could in theory make eleven tricks but if you adopt a routine line of defence, declarer will play safely for ten tricks. Suppose you win the second diamond and shift to a spade or a trump. Declarer will play a top trump, cross to dummy in spades and lead a trump, playing low if you follow low. This safety play guards against your holding Q-J-x-x. It would not help you to split your honours on the second round of trumps.

To defeat the contract, you need to persuade declarer that the safety play is too risky. Declarer will forego such a safety play if there is a danger of a ruff and so you should overtake the queen of diamonds with the king, cash the ace of diamonds and then switch to the two of clubs at trick 3. You are trying to create the illusion that you have a singleton club.

If declarer falls for the bait, declarer will reject the safety play and will lay down the ace and king of trumps. You will then score two trumps, two diamond tricks and a story on which to dine out for weeks.